Dear A
Nom
Travel - you'll still be a Texan!
Love
Uncle Bailey

THE MIGRATION TO TEXAS: BLOOD, SWEAT, AND TEARS

(THE EVOLUTION OF THE TEXANS)

ISBN 978-1534919907

THE MIGRATION TO TEXAS: BLOOD, SWEAT & TEARS

(The Evolution of The Texans)

Bailey D. Reynolds

CONTENTS

CHAPTER   **PAGE**

1. A trickle of immigrants come to the New World   16
2. England in the 1500's - 1600's   23
3. Ireland in the 1500's – 1600's   26
4. Scotland in the 1500's – 1600's   30
5. Christopher Reynolds – 1600's   32
6. Jobe Whitlock – 1600's   40
7. The Colonies in America – 1600's   46
8. Cortez' Conquest of Mexico 1519-1521   53
9. American Colonials move South and West   58
10. Louisiana Purchase   61
11. Mexico Defeats Spain   64
12. Americans begin to colonize Tejas   66
13. Tejas Settlers battle Indians   72
14. Conflict Between Settler3s and Mexico   80
15. Future Leaders Emerge   89
16. The Battle For The Alamo   104
17. Victory at San Jacinto   109
18. Texas wins –Now it is a Republic   117
19. Ethnic Immigrants begin to Arrive in Texas   134

20	Richard King and Mifflin Kenedy	145
21	The Texas Rangers	150
22	The Annexation of Texas	161
23	War and Peace	169
24	War Clouds Gather	178
25	The War Between The States	181
26	Texas Joins The Confederacy	187
27	Reconstruction And Martial Law	194
28	Texas Strived To Return To Normalcy	202
29	Ethnic Immigrants put their stamp on Texas	211
30	Goodnight Loving Cattle Trail	222
31	A Blowout Shakes Up Texas	226
32	Texas Rangers Get Their Man	231
33	Texas Ranches And Ranchers	234
34	Texans And Politics	242
35	A Few Claims to Fame	247
36	Some Texas "Old Coots"	255
37	A Few Texas Ladies And Icons	273
38	A Few Native Sons	278
39	And A Few Really Successful Entrepreneurs	285
40	Just A Few Texas Artists Of Note	292

41 And A Few Texans Of Renown	297
42 More To Texas Than The Wild West	303
43 Riding Off Into The Sunset	309

THE EVOLUTION OF THE TEXANS

PROLOGUE

"Texas". There just seems to be an aura about the name; and more especially about the place and the people attracted to its land. Texas, and by extension, the word "Texans", is as well, or better known world-wide, than many sovereign nations. The very idea of such notoriety for a physical place and its native citizens on our planet may give one reason to pause and to wonder why?

By some accounts, many people in America and elsewhere, are of the opinion that Texas, and especially native Texans, are "different". They seem to feel that Texans have an aura about them, a philosophy and an attitude different from people who have come to Texas from other states and countries. There appears to be a consensus of opinion, that even though we do speak the English language, we speak it differently than people from other parts of America. To others, Texans appear to be "arrogant" (interpreted by us Texans as self reliant and assured) "brash", (interpreted as friendly and outspoken), "uncivilized", (interpreted as well adapted to their surroundings), "chauvinistic", (interpreted as nice to other people, especially to ladies), and "ferociously independent", (interpreted as minding their own affairs and hoping others do the same). I can find no good reason to disagree with these opinions, (as interpreted by us Texans). It is a question that has nagged at me for the better part of fifty years. This opinion about Texans does not appear to be a fleeting phenomenon, but one that seems to be universally held, not only by Americans living in other states, but by a majority of people visiting our state, and even those who have migrated to Texas and have made their home here.

Some years ago I discussed the matter a number of times and at some length with a good friend who was originally from another state. At the time he was the

Managing Editor of several daily newspapers and traveled extensively about the state and frequently met with academics who are native Texans. He agreed with the premise that Texans are "different" but he was unable to satisfactorily explain exactly how Texans were different, nor why he came to have that opinion. If it is an accepted fact that Texans are different, and a vast number of "non-Texans" do accept it as fact, there must be a compelling reason for this to be so. My friend encouraged me to do some research and to follow my instincts about where to search into the reasons or cause of this anomaly. He assured me that what I was to begin, if completed, would be a worthwhile historical note for present and future Texans' descendents. To me, it appeared to be a reasonable and a personal challenge.

Some fifteen years ago, after retiring for the third time and with time to spare, I decided to begin my research on the matter. One of the first important realities in Texas history, is the home state or country of origin of many of the very earliest Texans. It quickly became clear that to do any research that would ultimately be of some consequence, I would have to explore past American history for at least the last three hundred years, even as far back as the original pilgrims. It was fortunate for me, and very agreeable with my wife, for it be necessary to research my project from both sides of the pond. We spent considerable time and multiple trips crossing the pond, to Ireland, Northern Ireland, Scotland and England. When the Irish, Scots and the English discovered why we were doing our research, they "jumped in with both feet" to help us. They love Texans! (We quickly discovered that it would be to our advantage to introduce ourselves and immediately add "We're from Texas!" It usually got their attention). The deeper we delved into it, the more intrigued both of us became. It became a passion that we felt compelled to pursue in an effort to explain the matter, and if not supported by facts, put the matter to rest, at least in my own mind.

To begin from a firm foundation, we began doing research on why my own ancestors, on my father's side, who were originally from Canterbury, County Kent, in England, and immigrated to America in 1621, and ultimately to Texas, and my ancestors on my mother's side, (Whitlock), who came from Belfast, Northern Ireland. We soon discovered that we would have to dig a bit deeper into the history of the ancestry of the earliest immigrants to America, including some of my ancestors. This is not to be a history of my ancestors, but I chose their migration to America as a starting point in time and as an example of the hardships and experiences of an average immigrant during that time period. My intent is to bring forth vignettes of history and our ancestors who have had an important influence on us Texans.

Our initial research began with the first immigrants that settled the original thirteen colonies;

the Pilgrims who immigrated from England. We soon noted that following the two great famines in Ireland, 1740-1741 and the Great Potato Famine of 1845-1852, the largest migration of settlers ever to come to America up until that time came from Ireland. During and following the famines, there were more than one million Irish immigrants seeking to make new lives in America. One has only to visit the centuries old cemeteries of Ireland and note the ages on tombstones of infants, adults up to fifty and sixty years of age or more; both mothers and fathers, grandmothers and grandfathers, aunts and uncles, all of one family, who died within a few months of one another during the famines, to understand the panic that caused many of the Irish to immigrate to America. Many Scots-Irish immigrated from both Scotland and Northern Ireland during this same period. Some little known facts about our Irish and Scots-Irish ancestral heritage:

- 27 Million Americans can trace their ancestry back to the Irish, Scots and Scots-Irish.
- Nine of the 13 governors of the original colonies were Scots-Irish.
- Of the 56 signers of the American Declaration of Independence 26 were Irish, Scots or Scots-Irish; there were 27 English, 2 Welch, and 1 Finn.
- In 1776, the year of the American Revolution, statistics of the time show that of the white population in the Colonies,, 85% were a combination of English, Irish, Scots-Irish and Scots. .

As our research evolved and we progressed to the period in history of the colonization of Texas, we began to delve into the ancestry of the early principal leaders who influenced the history of Texas. We were amazed to discover that almost to a man, (and no doubt, their women) they were of either English, Scots, Irish, or Scots-Irish ancestry. A large number of the men important to our history, for example; Stephen F. Austin, Sam Houston, Davy Crockett, William Barrett Travis and James Bowie were all of Scots-Irish ancestry. This is not to say that there were no other ethnic groups that came to Texas in its early history, but a majority of the original trail blazers and settlers were from England, Scotland and Ireland. In view of the conditions in their home country, there can be but little doubt why these determined people, from both England, Scotland and Ireland, with the courage and ability to make the arduous journey to the New World, chose to do so. Only the strongest, the most resolute, had the courage to make the supreme sacrifice. Those folk were the ancestors of the Texans.

When the colonization of Texas began, it was not sanctioned, promoted, financed, or protected militarily by any government. Texas was a part of the Spanish, and later, the Mexican empire. The pioneers of Texas were totally and completely on their own. They had to overcome the natural elements, the Indians, and the privations of a wild country with no hope of aid or assistance from anyone or any government. Survival in this land was literally the "Survival of the Fittest". No other state or territory was as ignored and disregarded as was Texas. No other state had to fight a forty year war for survival against hostile Indians, the disadvantages of an arbitrary and irresponsible foreign government as did Texas, even for many years after annexation into the United States

Those strong, independent and courageous immigrants who settled the original thirteen colonies, were theTexans' immediate ancestors; descendents of hardened survivors who were wise enough in their struggles to have outlasted a large percentage of their contemporaries. They were forced by circumstances to make important and far reaching decisions, often with very little experience and very little time to educate themselves on the subject. Amazingly, most of their decisions, made under difficult circumstances, proved to be intelligently made. Many of those decisions affect us even today. Those early immigrants were a few of the strong individuals who formed the Texans' heritage, character and philosophy for their descendents who influenced us to become who we are today.

CHAPTER 1

A TRICKLE OF IMMMIGRANTS TO THE NEW WORLD BEGINS

The history of the immigration of the early pilgrims who settled the original 13 colonies, their determination to create a new life in a new country, literally hacked out of the wilderness with their bare hands, is the beginning of the story of the evolution of the Texans. Those immigrants were our forefathers. Only through that background is it possible to understand why we are who we are.

By the fourteenth century, man had acquired the knowledge and the art of navigation and other skills that allowed him to travel not only over land, but the seas as well. As man's knowledge and skills increased, his love of and greed for material possessions increased proportionately. Fast on the heels of greed is the human desire for freedom in his pursuits. When Queen Isabella of Spain financed Christopher Columbus in the outfitting of his ships to sail in search of new lands, it was not a humanitarian project, rather it was the prospect of additional riches for her Spanish treasury that inspired her. Once the new world was discovered, a Pandora's Box was opened and the lid could never again be closed.

There is no record of any effort by Queen Isabella of Spain, or her government, to colonize this new found land. Centuries later, a similar situation would exist in "Tejas", (pronounced Tay-Haas). Also, according to history, the first serious attempt to colonize America was by the English when in 1620 the Pilgrims landed on the shores of Cape Cod Bay.

When the original colonists first arrived in the new world, the indigenous Indians welcomed these new immigrants with peace and hospitality just as they had Christopher Columbus. They failed to realize that in a few years they would be over-run by many more immigrants with very different life styles and beliefs from their own. The original English colonists had little tolerance for the culture and religion of the Indians, whom they considered to be savages and heathens. The religion the Indians practiced was considered by the colonists to be pagan. As more and more colonists from Europe arrived in the New World, the Indian tribes were driven further and further from the lands of their ancestors. It was inevitable that the Indians would rebel. Within a few years fighting broke out between the colonists and the Indians. As more and more immigrants arrived, the strength of the colonists increased and the Indians were inexorably pushed further away from their native lands. Due to the diverse cultures of the colonists and the Indians, it is not surprising that the two peoples could never assimilate one culture with the other. Hostilities were inevitable and soon resulted in armed conflict between the white man and the red man. It was a conflict that was to continue for centuries, (later, even extending to Texas), as the European immigrants and the newly native born Anglo-Americans continually pushed southward and westward.

History books skim over the hard fact that America was literally born in conflict. America was actually carved out of the wilderness. Any effort to assimilate with the Indian culture, or their culture to ours, was doomed to failure from the start. Centuries later, the same would be true in Texas.

The earliest Pilgrims made the extremely hazardous journey to America in search of religious freedom and a life free of government coercion. Conditions in England were so intolerable as to cause the people to hazard such a dangerous voyage into the unknown. The perils of the voyage were well known. The sailing ships on which they crossed the huge Atlantic Ocean were cargo ships with very few, if any, facilities for passengers. The crews of many of these ships were a motley group of men consisting of felons, escaped prisoners, men fleeing from debt and the debtors prisons, and some were even pressed into service and forced against their will aboard the ships as crewmen. These ships were the sole mode of transport by which any immigrant, soldier, adventurer or pilgrim, could expect to travel to reach the new world. There was very little, if any privacy, and nothing to occupy their time to combat the boredom of the long voyage. On most voyages many different kinds and species of domestic animals were aboard the ships, so it is easy to imagine the sanitary conditions those on board had to contend with.

Depending upon the prevailing winds and weather, the treacherous voyage could take from six to eight weeks. There was no refrigeration or other means to prevent spoilage of meat, vegetables and other food supplies. What meat that could be preserved for the journey was salted pork packed in wooden barrels. The lack of fresh fruit, the major source of vitamin C, caused scurvy, the dreaded malady of the sailors and passengers at sea. The survival rate from scurvy, without access to vitamin C, was less than 50%. It was no surprise that the less hardy of these immigrants perished before they arrived in the new world. Only the bravest, strongest and most determined, of the immigrants were able to survive the hardships and hazards of the voyage. Sadly, during those early voyages, more immigrants perished at sea than made it to the new world.

Given those odds and circumstances, one wonders why these people took the tremendous risks required to reach these shores. Obviously it was not just for adventure or monetary reasons. Only the most dire circumstances at home, or an unrealistic view of how great the New World would be, or perhaps a combination of both, could have induced a majority of the immigrants to take the tremendous risks of the journey. It could only have been to escape intolerable conditions in their homeland. It seems obvious that these pioneers were not the meek, timid, weak of character, or the down trodden of spirit who took such improbable chances. These were hardy folk who desired a better life, freedom of religion and the opportunity to lead a life free of tyranny. They had enough faith in their own abilities to take the ultimate chance of their life. Our heritage and character lies within the ancestral genes of those brave people who dared take such unfathomable risks.

CHAPTER 2

ENGLAND IN THE 1500 & 1600's

Beginning in the 1500's King Henry VIII broke with the Catholic Pope in Rome.
Both the King and the Catholic Church in England were excommunicated from the Roman Catholic Church. The King issued a royal edict mandating the eradication of the Roman Catholic religion, or any religion other than the Church of England. This mandate continued throughout the reign of the next five monarchs. Catholics were severely persecuted and Priests were prohibited from holding Mass. During the reign of Charles I, religious and political unrest amongst the people became more and more intolerable. With the reign of Charles I, along came Oliver Cromwell, a strident puritan of the early Calvinist faith. Cromwell was elected to the Parliament as a member from his home constituency of Huntingdon in 1628 and again in 1629. He was then elected a third time as the Member from Cambridge in

1640 until 1642. Civil war raged between King Charles I and Parliament for several years. The King was imprisoned in the tower of London by the Parliament. Cromwell was appointed Lieutenant General and second in command of the "New Model Army" of Parliament where he gained a vast amount of influence and personal power in opposition to the King. He considered himself "God's Chosen Instrument" and his accomplishments to be the "will of God". The English Parliament conferred on him the title "The Lord Protector of England, Scotland and Ireland", and gave him very extensive powers over the realm.

He soon gained the support of a majority in the House of Commons and under his leadership King Charles I was tried and convicted for his "sins against his people". Cromwell was the 59th Member of Parliament to sign the order to execute the King.

King Charles I was beheaded in January, 1649. Cromwell immediately took over the English Parliament from 1650 until his death in 1658.

Cromwell harbored a hatred of Roman Catholics and he vowed to wipe out the practice of the Catholic faith in England and the Commonwealth or other protectorates, such as Ireland. He ruled through a captive parliament and instituted oppressive laws dictating the personal behavior of the citizens. Women were forbidden to wear "loud" clothing or facial cosmetics. Police patrolled the streets and when a woman was caught violating these edicts, she would be humiliated, often beaten, have her face roughly scrubbed, then be severely fined for the transgression. Cromwell even outlawed Christmas. Men were instructed to wear only black clothing. Religious days and rituals were dictated by law and citizens were required to observe them or face severe penalties.

CHAPTER 3

IRELAND IN THE 1500,s & 1600's

As much as Oliver Cromwell hated Catholics, he hated Irish Roman Catholics even more. In an effort to rid Ireland of Roman Catholicism, he sent army troops into southern Ireland. When the citizens of Wexford and Drogheda refused to surrender to his army, he ordered his troops to slaughter the entire population. In Drogheda his troops killed more than 3,500 of its citizens, including women and children, Catholic Priests and the helpless civilian prisoners they had captured. In the town of Wexford, on his orders, his troops killed over 2,000 Irish military troops and more than 1,500 civilians, including women and children, and burned the town. His troops were ordered to round up all surviving

Irish children left in the two towns to be shipped to the West Indies as slave laborers.

In the 17th century, the English government created, in what is now Northern Ireland, the "plantation system". By promising free land and subsidies, the government lured both English and Scots from Scotland to immigrate to these plantations in Ireland. The land, farms and homes were literally stolen from the Irish inhabitants. The English displaced thousands of native Irish people who were left with no place to go. These displaced people, primarily of the Roman Catholic faith, became serfs on their own land. Following Henry VIII's repudiation of papal authority over the Church of England, Ireland, by an overwhelming majority, had refused to accept the English Reformation. Consequently, under the English Government of Oliver Cromwell, the Roman Catholic religion in Ireland was outlawed and the English Anglican religion was forcibly imposed in both the Republic of Ireland and Northern

Ireland. In the Plantation area of Northern Ireland, (Ulster), the Calvinist religion, (Presbyterianism), preferred by Cromwell the national religion of Scotland, was imposed.

In order to hold any position of authority, an Irishman had to disavow his Catholic faith and accept the Anglican Church, or in Northern Ireland, the Calvinist faith, as his religion. This denouncement of one's religion was intolerable. It resulted in a hatred between the Roman Catholics and the Protestants and began a centuries long armed conflict between the two groups in Ireland. Many of these disenfranchised Irish, and later, many of the Scots-Irish from Ireland and Scotland would immigrate to America.

Not surprisingly, their descendents would become passionate fighters in America's struggle for independence and in the early struggle to eventually settle the land that was to become Texas. The parallel between the Irish and later the struggle of the Texans to break the chains of a tyrannical Mexican government and the freedom to worship as they pleased, is strikingly similar.

CHAPTER 4

SCOTLAND IN THE 1500,s & 1600's

The English and the Scots seemed to be perpetually at war. The depredations of war against the Scots by the English all but wiped out entire generations of Scots. Following Martin Luther's reformation movement on the European continent, the Calvinist movement was brought to Scotland by John Knox. Knox was responsible for the Presbyterian canons of worship. The Kirk system of governing the church became the national religious faith of Scotland. A system of persecution of Roman Catholics soon swept Scotland. Unable to practice their religion and stripped of most of their civil rights, many Scots longed to flee to America . Many Catholic families pooled what money they had and financed the voyage to America for one or two of the members of families who could not afford the cost, hoping that those family members could find employment in America and aid others in making the voyage.

A large majority of the early English and the Scots immigrants who came to America were of the Roman Catholic faith but there were also many Anglicans and people of other faiths in England, Scotland and Ireland, who were desperate to be free of the heavy yoke of religious repression, penury and oppression and go to America. In Scotland, the Jacobites, (partisans of King James I of Scotland), along with their Anglican and Presbyterian countrymen were prone to condemn "non believers and Papists, (Roman Catholics)", as heretics and frequently burned them at the stake.

CHAPTER 5

CHRISTOPHER REYNOLDS, COUNTY KENT, ENGLAND, 1600's

In England in the 1600's, it was a common practice when a boy child reached the age of twelve to fourteen years, to apprentice him to artisans, tradesmen, or businessmen, to learn a trade, usually with someone successful in their trade or endeavor. At eleven years of age, Christopher Reynolds the Younger, was apprenticed to Edward Shockley of London. Shockley was an old and trusted friend of the young Christopher's father George, and his grandfather, Christopher the Elder. Shockley was engaged in trade and commerce in London and Portsmouth. He owned several cargo ships that sailed between many of the various countries that supplied Shockley and his customers with various goods for trade. During his apprenticeship, Christopher Jr. had opportunities to travel to France, Africa and Ireland aboard ships operated by his employer. At the age of nineteen, while on a voyage to Dublin, Ireland, Christopher, Jr., met and fell in love with a beautiful lass, Elizabeth McCarthy of Belfast, Ireland.. Elizabeth was the youngest daughter of Jason McCarthy, one of the oldest and most well known Irish Catholic Clans in Ireland. Under the leadership of Oliver Cromwell the British had developed the Plantation System to lure the Scots and English land owners to Northern Ireland..They confiscated the lands of the Irish farmers and residents who had lived on those lands for centuries.

Unfortunately for the Irish, there had been no established system of legally recording land ownership in Ireland. Clans and families lived on the land, farmed, worked the soil, raised sheep, goats and cattle, with no thought of any need to record their ownership. Property was, by custom, transferred to the eldest son, and if no son was living, then to the eldest daughter. Everyone nearby knew what land belonged to whom, so their property rights were respected without question. In the absence of any legal proof of ownership, the British sent in armed English militia and forcefully removed the Irish from their rightful land, often leaving families and children penniless and with no place to go. Such was the fate of Elizabeth McCarthy's family. For those unfortunate Irish left with no home, it was not unusual for families fortunate enough to have relativities, no matter how far removed in relation, who could afford to and would accept the children and other family members into their homes. Fortunately for Elizabeth, she had an uncle in Dublin who was agreeable to accepting her into his family. Her uncle, Ian McCarthy, as well as the entire McCarthy clan, were devout Roman Catholics. Under English rule, the Catholic Church was outlawed in Ireland. On pain of punishment or even death, the Irish were required to denounce their faith to Catholicism and to pledge their allegiance to the British official church, the Church of England. Ian Mc Carthy and his family, along with Elizabeth, passively resisted the edict of the

British and refused to denounce their Catholic faith. Early in their relationship, Christopher Reynolds became aware of the dire straits of Elizabeth. He soon returned to Dublin where they were married. Christopher and Elizabeth returned to England, settling in County Kent, near Gravesend.

Soon after Christopher and Elizabeth established their home in southern England, Elizabeth became pregnant with their first child. Unfortunately, rumors began circulating about the area that Elizabeth was a practicing Roman Catholic; a "Papist". Soon the town folks began to openly shun the Reynolds and even began issuing threats against Elizabeth. The situation quickly became all but intolerable for both Christopher, who was extremely worried about his pregnant wife, and Elizabeth, who could no longer move about in the neighborhood without insults and threats.

Christopher had heard many reports from business associates and others who had been to America, about the great possibilities in the New World. He and Elizabeth agreed that their situation in England was becoming intolerable and they made the momentous decision to sail to America and a new life. In May 1632, they booked passage to America aboard the sailing ship, the "Francis and John", owned by Christopher's mentor and employer, Edward Shockley. Their perilous journey into the unknown, at least to them, was now to become a reality.

The ship was constructed as a cargo ship and only meager facilities were made available for creature comforts. The only private cabins aboard were for the captain and the first mate. In deference to Shockley, the ship's owner, and in consideration for Elizabeth's pregnant condition, the captain agreed to allow the Reynolds the use of his small cabin, certainly no luxury accommodation, but far better than those of their sixteen fellow passengers. The captain took over the mate's cabin and the mate bunked with the motley crew. The other passengers had to make do with nooks, corners and crannies, wherever they could find space to unroll their blankets, and prepare to spend up to six weeks, without sanitation facilities or privacy. Much of the cargo consisted of live stock and the stench aboard within a few days became all but unbearable.

The ship sailed out of the English Channel and into the huge Atlantic bound for America. Two days later as the ship passed the southern shore of Ireland,, in spite of a serious bout of sea sickness, according to her diary, " Elizabeth went on deck to sadly watch the mountains, hills and shore of her Irish home fade into the distance;" a homeland she was destined to never see again. Even in the early spring, the North Atlantic was no placid body of water. Frequent, violent squalls would hit the ship unexpectedly causing all but the hardiest of sailors to be violently sea sick. With no form of refrigeration aboard to preserve food stores, after three weeks at sea, fresh vegetables were exhausted, leaving a diet of mostly bread, water and salted meat. Scurvy was a common malady of sea going sailors. (Although the cause was not known in those days, it was caused primarily by the lack of vitamin C in their diet). Later ships stocked up with any sort of citrus fruit or other foods that were rich in vitamin C.. Along with many of the other passengers, Elizabeth quickly became sick with the malady. Unable to retain what food she was able to eat, it failed to furnish her with the nourishment a pregnant mother required. On the third day of her severe illness, she became violently ill and within an hour had miscarried her baby. The unborn child was buried at sea along with three fellow passengers, one man and two women. After thirty-four days at sea, the ship "Frances and John" sailed into the harbor of Norfolk, Virginia.

    Although Christopher had made previous arrangements for housing in nearby Suffolk, Virginia, Elizabeth was too ill to travel from Norfolk to their new home. She required several weeks to recuperate and forher to overcome the depression she suffered from the loss of her unborn child. Prior to leaving England, Christopher had directed an agent to acquire a 450 acre tobacco farm in Warwick County, Virginia. As soon as Elizabeth was physically able, they moved to the new property and began their life in America. Within a few years, Christopher and Elizabeth had seven healthy children; four boys, Christopher III, Richard, John, Thomas, and two girls, Elizabeth and Jane. These descendents of Christopher and Elizabeth Reynolds were to become important and solid citizens in the new world of America and their descendents were to play an important role in settling the future land that we now call Texas.

CHAPTER 6

JOBE WHOTLOCK, COUNTY ARMAGH

IRELAND, 1600's

In the early 1600's, James I, King of England/James VI, of Scotland, in an effort to increase the influence of the English Monarchy in Ireland, promoted the immigration of Scots to Northern Ireland by giving the Scots free land in Ireland. The land was confiscated from the Irish without any remuneration and given to the Scots, leaving the former Irish landholders homeless and with no place to go. Unknown to the Scotts immigrants, the land given to them and upon the fathers demise, did not pass to their descendents as an inheritance. Ownership was solely to the original Scotts occupier of the land. Under English law of progeny, land and estates passed through inheritance from father to the eldest son. However, the English Parliament altered the law as it applied to Ireland, eliminating the direct progeny, and at the death of the grantee, ownership reverted back to the King of England. The Scots-Irish immigrants were not aware of this part of the law and after settling on the land, working it and creating what they thought was an estate, upon the death of the father of the family, they suddenly discovered that the land and property they had worked so hard to acquire, no longer belonged to their family, but had reverted back to the King. Just as the English government had dispossessed the Irish from their rightful land, the Scots immigrants were likewise dispossessed and left landless and homeless.

Many of the Scots who immigrated to Northern Ireland were Roman Catholics, anxious to escape the harsh canons and strict puritan requirements of the Scotts Presbyterian Church. Once in Northern Ireland, they quickly discovered that their religious freedoms were even more restricted than they had been in Scotland. The new immigrants had to denounce their faith in the Roman Catholic Church and vow their allegiance to either the Church of England or the Presbyterian faith. Because of these onerous and rigid laws in Ireland, beginning in 1700, there was a mass exodus of the Scots-Irish from Northern Ireland to America; to the new world.

Jobe Whitlock and his brother Lot, immigrated from the Highlands of Scotland to Northern Ireland in the late 1600's and settled in County Armagh, where they both met and married Irish ladies. Both families had productive and successful farms. In order to conform to English law in Ireland. even though quietly retaining their Catholic belief and faith, they raised their families as Protestant church members. In 1701, Jobe was taken ill and died. After his death, the English government reclaimed his farm and other property, leaving his family homeless and all but penniless. Recognizing the hopelessness for the future of his family under the English law of progeny, Lot, the brother of Jobe, gathered up his family, consisting of his wife Ellen, four sons Jonathon, Angus, Daniel, and James, three daughters, Mary, Catherine, and Ellen, along with Jobe's family, consisting of his widow and her three sons and arranged passage to America.

They left behind all but the barest of necessities. They sailed from Belfast, Ireland destined to Charleston, South Carolina. Under the most favorable of weather conditions, the journey to America was always an arduous one. Unfavorable winds and several violent storms drove the ship far off course, adding more than a week to their trip. Drinking water was in very short supply and all fresh produce and food stuffs were soon exhausted, requiring severe cuts in food and water rations. Scurvy was already rampant among the crew and the two Whitlock families. Weakened by scurvy and the meager food rations, Jobe's widow and her four year old son died and were buried at sea.

After thirty-four days at sea, the ship finally made port at Savannah, Georgia, many miles south of their destination of Charleston, South Carolina. Rather than risk any more time aboard a ship at sea, Lot purchased two teams of mules and two covered wagons, loaded the families on board, and traveled overland to Charleston, a long and difficult journey. Upon arrival at Charleston, they discovered that the land agent they had delegated to purchase a farm near Charleston, had failed to do so and had absconded with their money that had been forwarded for that purpose. Almost penniless, Lot was able to find employment as a blacksmith and furrier in Charleston.

Jobe's oldest son, Jonathan, became an apprentice to a tobacco merchant in Charleston. His other children were able to find occasional work on farms in and around Charleston. By being frugal with his meager earnings, within a few years Jonathan was able to purchase a small tobacco farm near Suffolk, Virginia andreturn to farming. Tobacco farming was far different from farming in Ireland, where they raised primarily cereal and feed grains and the famous Irish potatoes. It took him several years of back breaking work before he had all of his land ready to plant. After several years and a small modicum of success was realized, Jonathon seriously began making plans to marry, settle down and raise a family. Jonathan Whitlock soon met Elizabeth Reynolds, daughter of Richard, the second son of Christopher Reynolds. They fell in love and were married. Their descendents were later to be a part of the migration to Texas.

CHAPTER 7

THE AMERICAN COLONIES, LATE 1600'S

In the new American colonies the English Anglican and Protestant immigrants were not much more tolerant of the Catholic faith than was their English sovereign, Queen Anne, (1602-1714). Her English Parliament issued the "Test Acts Restrictions" for the American colonies in1661. These laws required that all positions of government and authority in the American colonies be held only by persons of the Anglican aristocracy. This ruling was imposed upon the American colonies to effectively bar Catholics, Presbyterians, Methodists and people of other faiths from holding public positions of leadership. This law was one of the onerous burdens that had caused many of the colonists to migrate to the New World to begin with. They wanted to be free to manage their own affairs and to practice their respective religions. The American colonists complained so vociferously that the English Parliament finally exempted the colonies from its enforcement. However, the law would continue in effect in England until repealed by the English Parliament in 1828, long after America had won its independence.

The English colonists had brought with them their English culture, a part of which was their afternoon "tea". King George III had quickly recognized that the New World could bring sizable tax revenue into his dwindling treasury. As the heavy tax burden on the American colonies was increased by the English Sovereign, without any representation in the English parliament by the colonists, they rebelled against the Crown. Their anger caused them to dump a ship load of tea, just arrived from England, into Boston harbor. This rebellious act was the straw that would lead to the Revolutionary War.

King George and his English Parliament had paid little attention to their colony on the other side of the Atlantic Ocean. They certainly never appeared to fear any rebelliousness in their American subjects. When what they considered to be only a short, mild skirmish with a few rebellious colonists turned into a full scale war for American independence, it must have taken them some time to figure out that they did indeed have a war on their hands. But, never mind, their huge navy and "superior army" would surely settle the matter post haste and their colonists would have been taught their lesson. They were in for a surprise of major proportions. It is obvious that they had badly misjudged the temper and temperament of the colonists. They were facing colonies populated by an unusual group of people of various backgrounds who were already tried and proven by their experiences that had caused them to cross the ocean and establish a colony free of subjugation, colonists that in the years to come, were to develop the greatest and most powerful nation in the world.

General George Washington was of English ancestry. His family was considered to be of the English gentry, or of the aristocracy. One of his attributes was one of humility. Another, more important attribute was the ability to lead. At the beginning of the American revolution, General Washington had to be convinced that the revolution could succeed and that he was the man to lead a new, untrained army, into the battles ahead. Once convinced, he began pulling together an army of civilians, some of whom were also not totally convinced that the revolution could be successful, so it was up to General Washington to convince them of ultimate victory, which was not an easy task. A government had to be formed, an army to be armed with weapons and funds to be raised to feed and supply his army with the necessities as well as the weapons. The success of all of these requirements by the new revolutionists was to be the guiding light. for a future general facing the same tasks, General Samuel Houston of Texas.

General Washington's army was composed of a mixture of many diverse ethnic groups of men, not the least of which were the Irish and the Scots-Irish. The battles of Valley Forge and Yorktown are best remembered by American history, but an even more important but less well known battle was fought months earlier at King's Mountain in North Carolina's Piedmont Mountains. It was at King's Mountain that local militiamen, composed almost exclusively of Irish and Scots-Irish "Mountain Men", including Thomas Reynolds, a direct descendent of Christopher Reynolds, defeated a British Army Major, Major Patrick Ferguson, a mercenary Scotsman and a highly regarded officer. The English army was a force of more than thirteen hundred redcoats. Major Ferguson's defeat so demoralized Lord Cornwallis and the British army that he abandoned his effort to lead his forces into battle in North Carolina, a Patriots stronghold, and retreated into South Carolina where they were again defeated at the battle of Cowpens. Cornwallis' retreat to Virginia ended with his defeat at Yorktown and the end of the revolutionary war. The defeat of the English at Kings Mountain by the Piedmont Mountain men was the turning point of the Revolutionary War. Many of those Scots-Irish Mountain Men were descendants of the Ulstermen of Northern Ireland who had survived a one hundred and five day siege by the British at Londonderry, Northern Ireland many years before. War was not a new experience for them. Their victory over the British at King's Mountain served to solidify resistance against the Redcoats in all of the American colonies.

The Revolutionary War ended with General George Washington's defeat of the British under Lord Cornwallis in 1781 at Yorktown, Virginia. This feat is worthy of some reflection. George Washington and his small, mostly civilian Army, whipped the socks off both the Army and Navy of England. At that time, England was the greatest military power on the face of the earth. Washington and his small army of patriots accomplished a feat that not even the famous military genius, Napoleon

Bonaparte, Emperor of France, could do. These new Americans were just beginning to show the world the ingenuity, bravery and toughness for which they would become famous.

CHAPTER 8

CORTEZ' CONQUEST OF MEXICO

While the Colonists were busy settling and fighting for the American Colonies, Spain was also busy in the New World.

The first recorded history of Tejas dates from the 1500's. Hernando Cortez began his conquest of Mexico in 1518. The recorded history of Cortez' conquest was faithfully recorded by Spanish Catholic Priests. Their chronicles were meticulously translated and published in three volumes in 1871 by William G. Prescott. These recorded events were to play a very important role in the future of the land the Spaniards were to call Tejas.

In 1519, Spanish explorer and adventurer, Alonzo Alvarez de Piñeda, sailed down the Tejas Gulf Coast, creating the first known maps of the coast of "Tejas". Cabeza de Vaca shipwrecked on Galveston Island in 1528. A few years later he explored the southern portion of Tejas, (later to be called the "Wild Horse Desert") on his way to New Spain, later to be known as Mexico. In 1542, the Spaniard, Francisco Vasquez de Coronado, traveled across the northern part of what was later to become Texas in his quest for the Seven Cities of Cibola and their fabled gold. The gold he was searching for was not to be found in "Tejas".

The half-hearted attempts by Spain to colonize the territory of Tejas failed miserably. None of their outposts survived more than a few months at most. In 1813, Spain amended their immigration law to allow immigrants from the U. S. to come into Tejas in an effort to colonize the territory. To encourage American settlers to come and colonize the land, Spain offered a league of land (4,228 acres) to entrepreneurs to bring settlers to Tejas. The first grant was to Moses Austin of Missouri. At that time in history, Missouri was a colony of Spain. Austin, a citizen of one of Spain's colonies, was a very acceptable entrepreneur. Through the large Spanish land grant, Moses Austin, and later his son, Stephen F.

Austin and the earliest settlers of Texas had the encouragement of Spain but they had no financial support or military assistance from the Spanish government. By encouraging the early settlers to migrate to the area, Spain had hoped that the American immigrants would create buffer zones between their outposts along the Rio Grande and the hostile Indians north of their settlements in Tejas. Spain seems to have hoped and expected that the settlers would fight their fight for them, tame the wilderness and make the country safe and habitable without any cost or expense to Spain except for the nominal value of what land they granted the settlers.

Cortez and his Spanish adventurers, or Conquistadors, brought Roman Catholic Padres with them in their conquest of Mexico. As the Spanish began to explore north beyond the Rio Grande, they established numerous Catholic missions in parts of Tejas. The Padres attempted to convert the native Indians to

Catholicism but had little success to show for their efforts. A number of the Padres were actually killed and eaten by the cannibalistic Karankawa Indians.

    Prior to the conquest, Mexico was a land inhabited by native Indians. The Mayans, Aztec, and at least five other different, and distinct tribes, inhabited the various parts of the huge territory Cortez was to call "New Spain". The original purpose of his conquest was to search for gold and riches and to subjugate the natives rather than an attempt to colonize the land. As the Spanish galleons plied the seas between Spain and New Spain, laden with riches of gold and silver plundered from the conquered natives, they returned with Spanish adventurers eager to settle and make their fortune in New Spain. They did not come to settle and fight for their land, but to make their fortune, so they remained in the large, fortified cities and towns for their safety. These Spanish colonizers of New Spain made little or no effort to integrate the native Indians into the Spanish culture, but rather preferred to bend the will and culture of the natives to the Spanish way of life. The result was a bi-cultural society with the elite Spanish Grandees at the top and the "Mestizo", (those of mixed Spanish and Indian blood), at the bottom of the social ladder. Native Indians had no standing and were like so many cattle. To insure the continuation of this social division, any attempt to educate the native Indians, or Meztizos, was not only avoided but actively discouraged. It was a division that was to be continued well into the twentieth century. This societal division of the upper and lower castes of citizens was a system that would be foreign to the Anglo settlers who much later were to colonize Tejas. The Spanish Grandees were to be as contemptuous of the American settlers as they were of the native Indians.

CHAPTER 9

THE AMERICAN COLONESTS BEGIN TO MOVE WEST AND SOUTH

In the colonies all was not peaceful, but the "New Americans" had declared themselves and their country to be free of British rule. A new generation of Americans was born. A few of the New Americans, men like Samuel Houston, David Crockett, and Andrew Jackson, were men who were to play a large role in American and Texas history. Many were descendants of the English, Irish, and Scots-Irish Mountain Men. These were our ancestors. Among them were some of the descendants of Christopher Reynolds, Lot and Jobe Whitlock and their children. They were a people who had been tempered by years of conflict. These were a people who had at last begun to experience the wonders of freedom.

As the colonies grew, the more adventurous colonists began to blaze new trails to the south and to the west. Some moving as far west as the mighty Mississippi and others as far south as Tennessee and Northern Florida. The earliest colonists to the New World had had the encouragement, support, and financial backing of sponsors and at least a nominal hope, of military protection by the British government. The settlers of Texas, on the other hand, had no support, sponsors, financial backing, or protection of any organization or established government. They were literally "on their own". In other areas of the American frontier, settlers were most often preceded by Army troops that either drove the hostile Indians away or partially subdued them. The United States Cavalry foraged ahead of the western migration into Missouri, Kansas, Nebraska, Colorado, the Dakotas, Iowa, and later, the western territories, including Arizona, Nevada, and finally into California. The U. S. Army was making every attempt to protect the westbound immigrants. Forts were constructed as quickly as possible at frequent intervals as the westward migration moved farther and farther west, to provide as much protection as possible to the new settlers. Settlers who decided to head to Texas had no choice but to subsist on their own, defend themselves, make the land productive, or perish. It was only through the courage, hardiness and determination of the earliest settlers of Texas that the territory was made hospitable for future generations.

CHAPTER 10

.THE LOUISIANA PURCHASE

American frontiersmen and colonists did not begin to migrate south to Florida and the other southern states and westward toward Texas in large numbers, until France sold the Louisiana territories to the United States in 1803.

The French emperor, Napoleon Bonaparte was in dire need of money to pursue his war with England. Originally, the U. S. was only interested in that portion of the Louisiana Territory surrounding New Orleans and access to the Gulf of Mexico. Napoleon's offer of the balance of the Territory was much too attractive to pass up and the United States bought the entire Territory, paying less than six cents ($.06)per acre.

The French owned a portion of Texas that was only a small part of the Louisiana Purchase. By 1685, the French had claimed the area that they were to call "Louisiana", in honor of King Louis IV, from the east coast of Florida and west on the coast of the Gulf of Mexico, to the Red River and a strip of land north to the Canadian border. They had earlier begun casting their eyes westward and sent the French explorer LaSalle to plant the flag of France in the area the Spaniards called Tejas. La Salle established Fort St. Louis at Matagorda Bay, on the coast of the Gulf of Mexico, and laid claim to the territory for France. Within a couple of years LaSalle's men had tired of the harsh conditions. La Salle refused to abandon his enterprise so his men murdered him. Consequently, with no responsible leader to keep order, the remaining French explorers were soon eliminated by the hostile, Karankawa Indians. This brief foray gave France a tenuous claim to the small portion of the territory of Tejas. While Spain, and France claimed a portion of the territory, that now makes up the State of Texas, there were no Spanish or French settlers in this part of the territory. The indigenous inhabitants of this territory were multiple tribes of American Indians;

Comanche, Lipan, Karankawa, the Caddo, the Cherokee, and other tribes from Florida, Georgia, Alabama and Mississippi.

The Spanish needed to create a buffer zone between their eastern frontier and the new American territory to the north and east as a result of the American purchase of the Louisiana Territories from France in 1803. They hoped to accomplish this by enticing American immigrants with special land grants to settle in an area fifty-two miles wide all along their eastern frontier. This fifty-two mile wide swath of land lay generally west of the present day Louisiana state line and the Red River. It was anticipated that these settlers, by owning the land, would protect the Spanish eastern frontier against Indians and other intruders.

CHAPTER 11

MEXICO DECLARES INDEPENDENCE FROM SPAIN

The Mexicans won their independence from Spain in 1821. As a Republic, they had no better luck in their efforts to subjugate the Indians in the Territory now called " Tejas", than did the Spanish. Mexico made only tentative, half hearted attempts to colonize Tejas. Mexico had its own internal strife and paid little attention to the territory north of the Rio Grande.

Like Spain, Mexico badly needed to create a buffer zone between the hostile Indians of Tejas and their scattered settlements on the Rio Grande to protect their people and to free up their army to deal with internal strife. The unstable government of Mexico, needing military force to deal with the frequent rebellions and coups among its leaders, had no real desire to confront the Indians on their own. In order to create this buffer zone they needed immigrants. They gave serious consideration to luring immigrants from

France and Germany by offering them free land. The fear of a renewed presence by the French or the establishment of an aggressive German enclave that might owe allegiance to Germany, on the border of Tejas caused them to quickly reconsider. It appears that their hope was that American Immigrants, with ownership of the land, would be more amenable to Mexican rule. In 1821, the Mexican government amended their own law allowing American settlers to again migrate into the state of Coahuila-Tejas. Just as Spain had previously done, they began offering a league of land to American settlers, requiring them to live on the land, bring in an acceptable number of immigrants and to pledge their allegiance to Mexico. Thus began the attempt to colonize Texas.

CHAPTER 12

THE AMERICANS COLONIZE TEJAS

To be a colonist willing to move to Tejas took a tough new breed of early America pioneer. They were descendents of men and women whose talents, fortitude and patience had been tempered over more than two centuries. Men and women who had learned to fight for their rights, to overcome adversity, natural elements, to withstand the torturous treks through the wilderness, to survive hunger and pestilence and still have the desire to preserver. As the Western and Southern borders of America were expanded, descendents of the early families migrated to the south and west as these areas became accessible to the pioneers. As the pioneers moved forward into new lands, they established communities, villages and towns. Inevitably, at suitable places, some few members of these families stayed behind while others forged ahead into the unknown. My ancestors, the Reynolds' descendants, were no different.

They began their migration to America, landing in Virginia in the 1600's, and each succeeding generation moved farther and farther south and west. After the Louisiana Purchase in 1803, they, along with the other pioneers, had access to the southern territories of the present states of Florida, Alabama, Georgia, Tennessee, Louisiana, Texas and the Western Territories. On their way they fought and over-came hostile Indians, privations, sickness, tribulations, and deaths of loved ones. They continued to move ahead along with the other pioneers, settling and populating the new frontiers as they went, their descendants moving on to continue the migration. Predictably, some of them headed to Texas. It was debatable for many years whether the hard trek to Texas with the ensuing hardships, was worth the effort and sacrifice. If those colonists had foreseen the trials and tribulations they would have to endure, most likely they would have stayed home and Texas would still be called Tejas and still be a part of Mexico. but, in the true pioneer spirit, they came, they fought, they worked, and against all odds, they endured and eventually prospered. The hardships the early Texas settlers, had to overcome by their indomitable will and perseverance were formidable. Thus was shaped and molded the character of the "Texan". So it can be said that being a "Texan" is a result of genes, and a state of mind earned through hard work and experience. Some folks from other parts of the world perceive this state of mind as "brash", "arrogant", "prideful", "boastful", and "independent". Unfortunately, those folks don't know much about the history and the experiences of the Texans. Carving out a life and making a home in this harsh wilderness, fighting and winning a revolution against a repressive regime, establish a Republic, and finally an America state out of this unforgiving land, required a brash, independent people. It is understandable that a people who, when they have overcome these difficult struggles, may become prideful and boastful and a bit arrogant.

The name "Texas" is derived from the Caddo Indian word "Teysha", meaning "Hello Friend". The meaning of this word can almost universally be applied to Texans. Their hospitable nature may stem from the fact that Texas has been an eclectic society from the beginning, accepting the best of society and ignoring the rest. The early Texans were of many diverse cultures and societies, including English, Anglo-Saxon, Scots, and Scots-Irish and Mexican. Other cultures, including German, Polish, Dutch, French, Italian, Jewish, Czechs and other mixtures of Anglo-Europeans soon followed as Texas became safe and habitable. Each of these new ethnic immigrants added to the diversity and the culture of the new Texas. Most of the new immigrants tended to congregate with people of their own ethnic origin. As they settled different regions of Texas, they established towns and communities with others of their ethnicity. Many of the Texas towns established very early in the settlement of Texas are still populated by descendents of these early settlers.

Through marriages between the early pioneers the diverse religions and life styles melded into a totally new society and new cultures. It was primarily a society accustomed to European and American ways and laws. The early settlers brought with them little or no sense of prejudice or class distinction, except for those immigrant settlers who later came from the slave holding states of the deep South and who maintained their prejudices concerning the slaves. In the early 1800's, Moses Austin of Missouri received a grant of land in Tejas, located in the Spanish State of Couhuila-Tejas, from the King of Spain. Austin wasn't aware of it, but like the biblical Moses, and against all odds, he was leading his people to a promised land. After the death of Moses Austin, his son, Stephen F. Austin, came to Tejas to take over the land grant. The grant was transferable only by the Spanish government, therefore new authorization was required. Spain authorized the transfer of the grant from Moses Austin to his son, Stephen, but soon Mexico won its independence from Spain. In 1821, the grant was nullified by the government of Mexico.

It was again necessary for Austin to apply to the new government of Mexico to have it reinstated

Austin made several trips to the Capital of Mexico, Mexico City, D. F., to plead with the new Mexican Congress. He spent more than a year and a couple of stints in a Mexican prison before the government of Mexico ultimately granted him, in 1823, some 67,000 acres of land in the Mexican State of Coahuila-Tejas on the Brazos River. Much of this land today is a part of the area which is now the city of Austin, the Capital of the State of Texas.

CHAPTER 13

THE SETTLERS VS. THE INDIANS

Initially, the original colonists that Austin brought with him to Texas, had few problems with the native Indians. The first Indians these settlers encountered were the Caddo and the Lipan. The Caddo occupied the area of East Texas and the Lipan the area of Central Texas. Both of these tribes were agricultural and peaceful by nature. As more settlers came and began to move f urther west, they began to intrude on the hunting grounds of the plains Indians; the Apaches and the Comanche. As American frontiersmen moved south and into Florida, they began to displace the Cherokee. The American congress soon decreed that all Indians in Florida be moved to reservations in Oklahoma Territory. This forced migration of the Cherokee was later to become known as "The Trail of Tears" because of the loss of life of so many of the Cherokee en route to Oklahoma. Many of the Cherokee avoided Oklahoma Territory and managed to make their way to Texas, where they encountered the Apache and Comanche.

These tribes were nomadic warriors by nature who followed the huge herds of buffalo, deer, and other wild game that roamed the upper plains of north and west Texas. The buffalo provided the Comanche and the Apache, with meat for food, skins for shelter and bones that could be shaped into weapons. They were accustomed to fighting among each other as well as other tribes, to defend what they considered their rightful hunting territory. As the Cherokee moved into these hunting lands the buffalo became scarce, causing serious problems between all of the Indian tribes. The battle for food began to drive the Indians to raiding the settlers. Serious problems were ahead.

The early Spanish Conquistadors had introduced the Spanish horse, or mustang, into Texas two centuries earlier. Once captured and domesticated, the horse gave the Indian a tremendous advantage in their hunting ability as well as making them formidable foes in their battles with their enemies. Astride the bareback horse, the Indian warrior could run down the buffalo rather than stalking them on foot. Both the Comanche and the Apache and later the Cherokee, became excellent horsemen. They were able to shoot their arrows with superb accuracy from horse back and to wield their lances with deadly consequences to their target. These Indians considered the wild prairies and high plains their home. They were determined to defend their territory against all intruders, whether they be other Indian tribes, the Mexicans, or the Anglo settlers. Indian warriors were considered to be primitive by the colonists, but were ferocious foes and fought with skill and cunning.

The Indian's religious belief was considered superstition by both the Mexican Catholic Padres and the Anglo settlers. The rituals of the Indians centered around the natural seasons of the year, the moon, the stars and the sun. It was a religion that was foreign to the religious faith of Catholics and Protestants alike and was looked upon as both pagan and barbaric. With the exception of the cannibalistic, Karankawa Indian Tribe, native American Indians are not known to have used human sacrifices in any of their rituals. The Indian worshipped the sun as his Father and the moon as his Mother. They considered the Giver Of All Good, the "Great Mystery". Their belief taught them that it was their duty to be courageous in war and adversity, to be generous to friends and faithful to comrades. Indian warriors performed great feats of bravery in recovering their dead or wounded comrades from the field of battle. They were taught to save their comrades from their enemies and to give those slain in battle a decent burial with their scalp intact in order to enter "The Happy Hunting Ground", their equivalent of our Heaven. They were truly a formidable foe the early settlers encountered as they attempted to settle the prairies and plains of Texas.

When the American frontier began to grow, moving into the deep south, especially Florida, the American frontiersmen began to displace the Cherokee from their lands. As the Cherokee were being driven from their native lands by the Americans, they were forced further and further west and eventually into Oklahoma Territory and Texas. Accustomed to forested lands and the humid coastal lands, the Cherokee now faced the barren, dry, semi-desert lands of the Texas plains. Pursued by the American soldiers and facing the hostile tribes of the Texas plains Indians, the Cherokee were left with no choice but to fight for their survival. Not only did they have to fight the other Indian tribes, but also the Texas settlers for the Buffalo and use of the land. Very soon, the Cherokees, like the Comanche and the Apaches, began raiding the Texan's homesteads. The warfare between the Indian tribes and between the Indians and the Texas settlers was vicious, brutal and barbaric. It quickly became a battle in which not either side could give any quarter. It was fight and win or fight and die. Survival of the fittest was a fact of life for the Texans as well as the Indians.

As settlers in Texas moved westward onto the prairies and plains, the homesteads were more and more isolated. Very often it would be a full day's ride on horseback to the nearest neighbor. There being no useable timber available, most of the primitive houses were dugouts, half underground with the exposed portion covered with mud, brush, and grass roofs, or constructed of logs or saplings, and the cracks filled with a mixture of mud and grass, called wattle. The work was backbreaking for both the men and the women, and for the children, as soon as they were old enough and strong enough to make a contribution. Each member of the family was required to do a share of the work. The women and girls had the task of cooking over a hot, wood stove or open fire, washing the clothes, which most often required them to carry water for considerable distances from a creek, river, or well, or to carry the clothes to the creek or river tobe washed on rocks and hung to dry on bushes or tree branches. It was also customary for the women of the family to tend a garden from which they harvested their vegetables. The men worked from dawn to dark, either farming or tending cattle, goats or sheep, and keeping what equipment they had in good repair. Their houses provided very little security against marauding Indians. With the men away from their homes all day working, the women and children were left unprotected. Many pioneer women became excellent shots with a rifle, but a single shot rifle was little protection against a band of Indians with their horses, lances, bows and arrows and their sharp knives. Unable to escape and with little expectation of help from their husbands or neighbors, many of the wives and children of these early settlers were either killed and scalped or taken captive by the Indians. As the incidents of marauding Indians increased, the settlers began forming loosely-knit bands of militia to track and try to destroy the warriors; and if possible, to rescue their women and children, and to destroy the Indian encampments.

It was inevitable that the settlers, who were by nature of independent spirit, but accustomed to some protection from marauders, would have an inherent resentment against the failure of any government that failed to protect them. They would soon come into conflict with the incompetent rulers in Mexico City.

CHAPTER 14

CONFLICT BETWEEN THE SETTLERS AND MEXICO

During the colonization of Texas the colonists were primarily of a protestant faith. They were surprised and disappointed to learn that to be allowed to own property and to plan a permanent future in Tejas, they would be required by the Mexican government to convert to the Catholic religion and swear their allegiance to Mexico. They were also soon to learn that although they could own property, they could not vote and had no say in Mexican government. Many of the colonists publicly converted, but in general terms, did so for the sake of appearance only, and to comply with Mexican law. Most continued to practice the religious beliefs they brought with them to Texas. These restrictive requirements of Mexican law was a constant thorn in the side of the colonists; a requirement that was somewhat alleviated when Mexico enacted a new constitution in 1824, limiting the ownership of property by the Catholic

Church and freeing the people to worship as they chose and to legally own property. Within two years, another revolution changed the government in Mexico City again and under the new President, General Santa Anna, the constitution reverted back once again to the old laws. Such ijnconsistancy in the Federal Government was sowing the seeds for rebellion.

In 1829, Santa Anna, the President of Mexico sent his brother-in-law, General Manuel Teran to inspect the province of Coahuila-Tejas. He reported back to President Santa Anna, "with alarm at the strength, independence, and swaggering arrogance of the Americans". He declared that "they had little respect for Mexican law, and that each one carried his political constitution inis pocket, and assumed that he was a sovereign in his own right". As a result of Teran's report, and fearful of the independence and disregard of Mexican laws by the Texans, at the insistence of the President, the Mexican congress passed a law in 1830 prohibiting further immigration of Americans into the state of Coahuila-Tejas. From this report of General Teran's, it was apparent that "Texans" were already considered "independent" and "arrogant". (At no other place or time in our research of early Texas history have we found Texans to be referred to in those words or in such a manner).

Just as American immigration laws in the twentieth and twenty-first century have proven ineffective in halting the immigration from Mexico moving north across the border into Texas, so the Mexican immigration laws of the eighteenth century did little to slow the movement of Americans southward into Tejas, then a Mexican territory.

The immigrant settlers repeatedly pledged their allegiance to the government of Mexico but paid little attention to Mexican law and customs. Under Spanish rule, Mexico was governed, (and still is), under the Napoleonic Law. The accused is guilty until proven innocent; trial was by a tribunal rather than a Judge and a Jury, there was no habeas corpus and the accused could be jailed and held indefinitely before being brought to trial. Following its independence from Spain, the Mexican Republic retained this same code of law.

The Anglo settlers were accustomed to the laws of the United States with all of the accompanying rights, especially the right of habeas corpus, or protection against illegal detention, trial by a jury of their peers, legal representation, freedom to assemble, and freedom of religion. The settlers were already incensed by the incarceration for over a year, of Stephen F. Austin in Mexico City in 1834, where he had gone for the second time, to renew his grant of land in Texas. Mexico, following its independence from Spain, required that land grants issued by Spain, had to be re-confirmed by the Mexican Congress. Following their war with Spain, the new congress was in total disarray and remained so for many months. Stephan F. Austin had come to Mexico

City, D. F. to make his application for Mexican confirmation of his grant, but was rebuffed in his attempts. Realizing the importance of the land grant, he stayed on and continued petitioning the Mexican Congress. For some unknown reason, the Mexican government had him imprisoned. Austin was in solitary confinement for almost the full year, without any charges being filed for any violation of Mexican law. After more than a year the Mexican congress approved his grant and he was released, without any explanation for his confinement.

Many of the laws and regulations of the Republic of Mexico were capricious and frequently arbitrarily enforced. Even so, so long as the settlers were left alone, they were content to be self governing and to pay lip service to the edicts of the Mexican government. As alien and as burdensome as the laws were to the settlers, they continued to pay allegiance and affirm their loyalty to the Mexican government. But they repeatedly petitioned for the repeal of the Mexican decree of 1830, limiting immigration of settlers from the north. Although the settlers were exempt from customs laws for several years after their arrival, other Mexican laws were often unfairly enforced by inexperienced Mexican political appointees pressed upon the settlers by the Mexican Government. They were not allowed to vote in the elections that the Mexican government held from time to time. The settlers wanted some say over the election and appointment of the civil authorities charged with enforcing the laws under which they were being governed.

The Anglos did not understand the culture of the Mexicans, nor did the Mexicans understand the culture of the Anglos. As a result, the Texans were slow to assimilate into the Mexican culture and the Mexicans slow to assimilation into the Anglo culture. This situation was viewed with great apprehension by the Mexican government. The Texans, for their part, grew more and more resentful of Mexican rule. Tejas was a part of the state of Coahuila-Tejas and the Texans were pressing for autonomous statehood separate from Coahuila. The Texans were accustomed to the power of the government emanating from the people upward to the head of the government, and the Mexican culture was based on the power of the government lying with the head, either President or Dictator, and at least some small semblance of government, emanating downward to the people. Although elected by the people, the President of the Republic of Mexico was all powerful and ruled with dictatorial powers, often only with the support of the army. It was inevitable that serious differences would arise between the two cultures.

From the time of their independence from Spain, the Mexican government had been in total disarray. The government and most of the laws were patterned on the type of government and rule of law inherited from Spain. In 1829, at Tampico, General Santa Anna had defeated the last and final effort of Spain to re-conquer

Mexico. Santa Anna emerged from the battle a national hero. Riding on the swell of his popularity, he was elected President of Mexico. While Santa Anna publicly espoused reform and a restoration of power to the states, his true goal was to centralize all power with the president. He was little more than a military dictator backed by the might of the Mexican army. He had no intention of allowing Tejas to separate from Coahuila and to become an autonomous state. He viewed the Texans as too independently minded to be trusted to govern themselves.

In 1834, President Santa Anna replaced the state government of Coahuila-Tejas with hand-picked appointees; people who had no experience or talent in governing. The result was chaos and resentment by the Texans. Mexican General Cos, Santa Anna's brother-in-law, was sent to Tejas to beef up and reinforce the garrisons at San Antonio, Goliad, Velasco and Anahuac. General Cos had no time nor patience for the complaints of the settlers. He recommended that the garrisons at all four Mexican posts be considerably increased and that cannon be installed at each outpost.

The Texans had begun to grow weary of the despotism and chaos that had existed within the Mexican government for years and was growing steadily worse by the day. They were especially incensed by the installation of cannons at the various Mexican Forts. A full scale rebellion would break out within a matter of months.

CHAPTER 15

FUTURE LEADERS EMERGE

The success of any worthwhile endeavor will always be governed by the abilities, intelligence, experience, foresight, and tenacity of its leaders. In this regard the early settlers of Texas were indeed fortunate. Unfortunately, a number of the bravest of these early leaders were to fall in battle during the earliest days of the revolution.

Most of the settlers were, by nature, hard working individuals and independent citizens who were seeking a productive land on which to build their homes and futures. It is truly remarkable that any women had chosen to brave the conditions of the early settlers. The sons and daughters of these remarkable men and women endured this harsh life. They were respectful of their family responsibilities and the land that was so dearly won. It was crucial for these ordinary citizens to have intelligent leadership; leaders that had the vision to see beyond the day-to-day drudgery required for a mere existence. Even after the settlement of Tejas by the Americans, while under Mexican rule there was no opportunity to exercise such leadership. Fortunately, although none of them knew it at the time, such leaders were in the vanguard of men that settled Texas. Their names are forever enshrined and intertwined in the history of Texas. The brave and intelligent General George Washington is almost universally considered to be the father of the United States of America. Likewise, although not born into the aristocracy, Samuel Houston did for the Republic of Texas what Washington did for America. Both men had similar experiences in their life. Both men were born leaders and almost universally respected by their peers. Much as Washington had done, Houston led a small army against a much superior enemy force and won. He fought for the Texans liberty and freedom from tyranny and he led the people through the most trying period of the new Republic. Houston's contributions to and influence up on the history of Texas is a subject that deserves considerable attention. His genealogy and family history, his early years and his experiences, guided him in his recommendations for the formation of the new Republic. All were influences that would reflect on the character and future of Texans.

Samuel "Sam" Houston was born at Timber Ridge in the Shenandoah Valley of Virginia. He was of Scots-Irish descent. His great-great Grandfather was Sir John Houston, a native of Scotland. His grand-father, John, emigrated to Ulster, Ireland during the English Plantation period of the late seventeenth century. Unable to inherit an estate and facing a bleak future in Ireland, John Houston and his family emigrated to the American colonies in 1735. He soon moved his family, along with a number of other Scots-Irish migrants, to an enclave of a larger number of other Scots-Irish migrants in the Shenandoah Valley of Virginia. There a son, Samuel's father, Robert Houston, was born. Samuel Houston was born March 2, 1793, the fifth son of nine children. His Father, Robert Houston died in 1807 after having purchased land in East Tennessee. He passed away before he could move his family to their new home. Sam's mother Elizabeth, moved the family to the property in Maryville, Tennessee when Sam was 14 years old. At age 16, Sam, disliking work as a clerk in his brother's store, ran away from home and lived with a Cherokee Indian tribe until he was 19. He became fluent in the Cherokee language.

In 1812, Sam joined the 39th infantry regiment to fight the British in the war of 1812. He was soon promoted to lieutenant and was wounded by bullets in his shoulder and arm. A disabled veteran, he went to New Orleans, Louisiana for surgery and convalescence. In 1817, he served briefly as a sub-agent for his mentor, General Andrew Jackson in the removal of the Cherokee Indians from East Tennessee to Arkansas Territory.

In 1818, Houston studied law for six months and passed the bar examination in Tennessee. He was appointed local prosecutor in Nashville, Tennessee. He was elected to Congress from the state of Tennessee and served two terms, from 1823 to 1827 in the American House of Representatives. During this period as a Congressman, he met and became friendly with David Crocket, another Tennessee Congressman. He then ran for and won, the office of Governor of the State of Tennessee. In January 1829, he married but was quickly divorced after only a few months. He had planned to run for a second term as governor, but following his divorce he was very distressed and resigned from the office.

In late 1829, depressed over his failed marriage, he went to Arkansas and again lived with a Cherokee Indian tribe. In 1830 and again in 1833, he was elected to the House of Representatives. Houston went to Washington to protest and expose the frauds of government agents against the Cherokee. While in

Washington, he became embroiled in a physical controversy with a Congressman from Ohio and beat him with a walking cane. The Congressman pulled a pistol, but it miss-fired. Houston was tried by Congress and convicted of conduct unbecoming a United States Congressman, but only lightly reprimanded. He was fined $500. in civil damages. Houston immediately left Washington, D. C. and headed for Tejas, then a part of Mexico. When he reached Tejas he found the country in great turmoil. There was very serious debate on the matter of rebellion and declaring Tejas a sovereign state, free from Mexico. Relying on his political experience in Tennessee, the Texans appointed him to the convention that was considering independence from Mexico. He was chosen to attend two conventions, one in 1833 and again in 1835, called to discuss Texas' independence from Mexico. At the convention in 1836, Texas finally declared its independence, on March 2, 1836, Houston's 43rd birthday. He was one of the signers of the Texas

Declaration of Independence. The convention named Sam Houston Commander-in-Chief of the Army of the Republic. Sam Houston would be the General to lead the Texans to independence at the battle of San Jacinto. He proved to be one of the most influential leaders in the formation and administration of the government of the Republic of Texas. His military experience and knowledge of politics served both him and Texas well in the years ahead.

    Stephan F. Austin was born November 3, 1793 in southwestern Virginia to Moses and Maria Austin. His family was of Irish heritage, his great Grandfather was born in Dublin, Ireland and emigrated to America among the early colonists. In 1798 Moses Austin moved his family to southwestern Missouri in what was then Missouri Territory and was under Spanish rule. At age ten, Stephen was sent to school in Connecticut, then spent two years at Transylvania University in Lexington, Kentucky. Moses Austin was engaged in the mining of lead and manufacturing. His son, Stephen, soon took over the management of the mining enterprise. For several years he was a member of the Missouri Territorial Legislature. While serving in the legislature he was appointed a Circuit Court Judge. In 1820 he traveled to New Orleans, Louisiana to study law. His father, Moses Austin went to San Antonio, in Mexican Tejas, to apply for a grant of land and as an impresario, permission to bring to Tejas and settle 300 families. Before Stephen could join his father in the enterprise, Moses died of pneumonia. Stephen proceeded on to Tejas and secured permission from Spain for a grant of land and permission to settle 300 families in Tejas. He continued to pursue the land grants and the emigration of American families as an Impresario under a license issued by the Spanish, and later the Mexican government. .

When Austin came to Tejas in 1821, at the age of twenty, he was experienced in business, the law, and politics. These were attributes that would serve both him and Texas well. Shortly after his return after more than a year in a Mexican prison, in late 1835, Austin was elected a delegate to the State convention considering a rebellion against Mexico. At the convention of 1836 Austin recommended all out war and a rebellion against Mexico which led to the Texans Declaration of Independence from Mexico.

James Bowie was born in 1790, of Scots and English ancestry, the son of a wealthy Louisiana plantation family. He was well educated for the times. He was schooled in the English language, in both reading and writing. He was also fluent in both Spanish and French. He earned quite a notorious reputation in the deep South as a duelist, killing several opponents, including the son of Jean Lafitte, the pirate. He became notorious for his prowess with a knife which led to the popularity of a large hunting knife, nicknamed "The Bowie Knife" In spite of his exploits, he was considered an honorable man and had the respect and admiration of both those in high society and those on the tougher, harsher side of life on the frontier. In the early 1800's he came to San Antonio and married the beautiful daughter of the Mexican Vice-Governor of Coahuila- Tejas. He became wealthy, owning several leagues of land and was an honored member of the Mexican society. His wife and children died during a cholera epidemic in 1833. In the meantime, Bowie had become friends with Sam Houston. With his ties to Mexican society gone, Bowie gravitated to the company of his Anglo-Saxon friends and soon became active and loyal to the revolution. He joined the struggle and when the revolution began, was with Sam Houston and his small army encamped at Gonzales. Concerned with the situation in San Antonio at the Alamo, General Houston dispatched Bowie there to analyze the situation and report back to him. Bowie, recognizing the precariousness and the problems with defending the Alamo, quickly decided to stay and assist in its defense.

David, "Davy" Crockett was born August 17, 1786 in Greene County, Tennessee. His Father was John Crockett of English, Irish and Scottish ancestry, He was the fifth of nine children. Davy's father was one of the Mountain men who fought in the Revolutionary War battle of King's Mountain in the Piedmont Mountains in the 1780's. As a young adult, Davy earned his living by hunting and trapping. He became a legend through his prowess with the long rifle. A Populist, he served as a Congressman from Tennessee in the United States House of Representatives. He came into conflict with President Andrew Jackson and his administration over budget matters, the inhumane expulsion of the Cherokee Indians from their lands in Florida, and the closure of the independent bank of the United States. Embittered by the administration's interference in the election which led to his defeat at the polls, Crockett made a short concession speech, telling his constituents to "Go to hell, I'm going to Texas". With twelve fellow Tennesseans, he kept his promise and came to Texas to join his friend Sam Houston. His experiences with the Indians, in politics, his prowess with a rifle and his indomitable will would serve him and Texas well within the next few years.

William Barrett Travis was of English descent. He was born in Saluda County, South Carolina on August 1, 1809. Well-educated, he taught school for several years, became an attorney at age 19 and practiced law in Alabama. Travis married in 1828 and had one son and a daughter. His marriage failed in 1831. He fled Alabama and migrated to Texas. Upon arrival in Texas in May 1831 he purchased land from Stephen F. Austin and set up a law practice in Anahuac, Texas. On December 19, 1835, he was commissioned as a Lieutenant Colonel in the Texas militia. He was ordered by General Sam Houston to recruit as many men as possible and to reinforce the soldiers at the Alamo Mission in San Antonio. He was skeptical about his ability to recruit enough men and to find arms and supplies to sustain them. He contemplated refusing to obey the order, but finally reluctantly agreed. Travis arrived at the Alamo on February 3, 1836 with eighteen men as reinforcements. As the senior officer, he was placed in command of the Alamo Garrison. To avoid friction with Bowie and his men, he shared the command with James Bowie. His education, military experience and leadership abilities would be invaluable to Texas in the very near future.

Benjamin, (Ben), Rush Milam was born in Kentucky October 5, 1788. His ancestors were Scots-Irish. His father was a Scotsman and his mother, Pattie (Boyd) Milam was of Irish heritage. Milam had little formal education. He joined the Kentucky militia and was elected a Lieutenant and served in the War of 1812. By 1818 he had moved to Texas and was engaged in trade with the Comanche Indians. In 1819 he traveled to New

Orleans where he joined an expedition to assist Mexico and the state of Coahuila-Tejas gain independence from Spain. In 1835, Milam traveled to Monclova, the capital of the Mexican state of Coahuila-Tejas in an effort to assist Texas settlers gain title to their land. While in Monclova, Milam learned that General Antonio Lopes de Santa Anna had overthrown the Mexican government and had established himself as President. Santa Anna, with the power of the Mexican army behind him, was a virtual Dictator. Hearing of the change in government, Milam desperately tried to return to Texas but was captured at Monterey and imprisoned. With the aid of several friendly Mexican guards, he soon escaped and dashed back to Texas. By chance he encountered a company of Texan soldiers en-route to capture Goliad where he learned of the efforts of the Texans to stage a rebellion against Mexico. They captured Goliad and some of the soldiers marched to help recapture San Antonio where the Texans previously had fought the

Mexican army of over 1,200 soldiers to a stand-still but then were over whelmed by sheer numbers. Upon arrival at San Antonio, Milam discovered that the Texans garrisoned at the Alamo at San Antonio were under siege by the Mexicans. He also learned that the Texan army had decided to abandon the siege and to return to Goliad and set up winter quarters. Milam returned with the Texans to Goliad. Realizing the fallacy of such a decision in Texas' fight for independence, when they reached Goliad, Milam made his famous plea to the soldiers: "Who will go with old Ben Milam back to San Antonio?" Three hundred men volunteered and all agreed to return and make an all out attack on San Antonio and the Alamo on December 5. Two days later, On December 7, during the battle for San Antonio, while studying the Mexican army's position across the river at the Alamo from atop the roof a house near the San Antonio River, Ben Milam was shot in the head and killed by a Mexican bullet. San Antonio was captured by the Texans on

December 9 and garrisoned their small army in the Alamo.

The Mexican's loss of Goliad and San Antonio, along with the Alamo, was to be the military action that resulted in the all out attack on San Antonio and the Alamo by Mexican General Santa Anna.

Meanwhile, in early March, 1836, Goliad was retaken by General Martin Perfecto de Cos and his army. San Antonio, was recaptured on February 23, by General Santa Anna. The Alamo fell to the overwhelming Mexican army on March 6, 1836.

CHAPTER 16

THE BATTLE FOR THE ALAMO

In Spanish the word Alamo, is the name for the Cottonwood Tree. When the Spanish Catholic mission at San Antonio was first established, it was surrounded by Cottonwood trees and, as a result, the mission was named "El Alamo".

Mexican General Antonio Lopez de Santa Anna, the President of Mexico, concluded that the pesky Texans were becoming too independent. He decided to take decisive action and remove the problem by overwhelming force of arms. The Mexican army, under General Santa Anna, moved rapidly northward and caught the Texans at San Antonio by surprise. The Alamo was placed under siege by the Mexican army on February 23, 1836.

On March 6, 1836, after the siege by General Santa Anna and his army of sixteen hundred well-trained and well equipped troops, the small, greatly outnumbered force of one hundred-eighty brave and gallant Texans, was overwhelmed at the Alamo. At the beginning of the siege, General Santa Anna posted a blood red flag atop the tower of the San Fernando Church, in plain sight of the defenders of the Alamo, signifying that no quarter would be given; no defender's life was to be spared. The Texans at the Alamo had ample opportunity to escape during the siege. Not one man fled, but elected to stay and fight, knowing that there was little, if any, probability of reinforcements and when they were overrun they would be facing a sure and horrible death. All one hundred eighty men, including the sixteen men Travis had brought to assist them, would soon be overwhelmed. All of the defenders were either killed in the battle or brutally slaughtered after they had surrendered to the Mexican army.

    Two women, their two children, and a black slave survived the siege: Susanna Dickinson, whose husband, Captain Almaron Dickinson was killed during the last moments of the battle, Her 2 year old daughter Angelina, along with Juana Navarro, whose husband was also killed during the last few minutes, her 2 year old son, and a black slave named Joe, all survived the battle unharmed. On orders from General Santa Anna, all of the surviving men of the battle, except Joe the Slave, including the wounded, sick or incapacitated, were massacred and their bodies mutilated. A few days after the battle, on General Santa Anna's orders, the two women and their children were allowed to leave San Antonio accompanied by the slave, Joe. They were told to warn any other rebellious Texans, especially General Sam Houston, that he, General Santa Anna, was bringing the Mexican army to destroy them all and put an end to their insurrection. Susanna and her group made their way more than 80 miles to Gonzales, Susanna's home town, where General Sam Houston and his small army was camped. She related the events of the siege to a skeptical Houston who had heard of the siege earlier in the day but refused to believe it. Susanna's two companions confirmed her story. Houston quickly made plans to evacuate Gonzales and recommended that all civilians also leave. Houston's suggestion sparked panic among the Gonzales citizens, along with the entire ad-hoc government of the new Republic who had sought refuge at Gonzales. They fled in what came to be known as the "Runaway Scrape". As soon as possible, Houston took his small army south in retreat until he could muster additional volunteers and train them to fight before confronting Santa Anna's army. Susanna Dickinson remained in Gonzales until her death in 1883.

CHAPTER 17

VICTORY AT SAN JACINTO

Just as George Washington is considered to be the Father of the United States of America, Samuel Houston, despite his circuitous journey, should be considered to be the Father of Texas.

In 1835, prior to the events leading up to the battle at the Alamo, Sam Houston, along with Stephen F. Austin, issued a call for all Texans to rebel against the tyranny inflicted upon them by the Mexican government. In the convention of March, 1836, the delegates declared the state to be an independent Republic. Sam Houston was appointed Commander-in-chief of the army. General Houston quickly organized a small citizens army of 374 poorly equipped, untrained and unsupplied Texans at Gonzales. While camped there with his small army, General Houston learned of the fall of the garrison at the Alamo from the two women survivors.

A few days after the fall of the Alamo, Colonel James Fannin and some 400 fellow Texans, garrisoned at the mission at Goliad, were overwhelmed by a superior force of a detachment of the Mexican army under the command of General Cos, the brother-in-law of Santa Anna, General of the Mexican army and President of Mexico.. After a fierce battle, Fannin and all of his surviving men surrendered under a white flag of truce. The terms of the surrender called for Colonel Fannin and all of his men to be taken as prisoners of war and to receive humane treatment. Within a day or two, General Santa Anna, ordered his brother-in-law, General Cos, to put all of the Texans before a firing squad. General Cos strenuously objected, but General Santa Anna refused to relent. Colonel Fannin and all of his men were massacred and their bodies left where they fell at the mission at Goliad.

After learning from Mrs. Dickenson, that General Santa Anna was marching with his large army toward his garrison at Gonzales, and that Goliad had fallen to the Mexicans, General Houston quickly began an orderly retreat, despite protests from his troops. General Houston advised the citizens of Gonzales and the few members of the ad-hoc government of Texas, to evacuate Gonzales and to seek sanctuary where-ever they could find safety from the marauding Mexican army. He stopped his army frequently during the retreat to train his troops as they moved south ahead of Santa Anna's army.

On the march south, almost 300 additional Texans joined Houston. At last Houston and his small army of about 700 men arrived at the bayous on the Texas gulf coast on the San Jacinto River. He knew they could retreat no further, but he also knew that Santa Anna was rapidly closing in on his position, making an escape impossible for the Mexican army as well. Houston established his lines of battle and prepared to meet his enemy. During the night, Santa Anna's weary soldiers made camp some few hundred yards in front of Houston's army. Late in the next afternoon Houston and his courageous men made a surprise attack on the Mexican army to the raging cry of "Remember the Alamo". It was a battle cry that rang loudly across the bayou at San Jacinto and continues to ring loudly whereever there is a battle involving American fighting men, more than 150 years after the battle of San Jacinto. The battle was over in less than an hour and the Mexicans began a disorganized retreat. The losses to General Sam Houston's army of less than 700 men were negligible with only two men killed and General Houston injured by a stray bullet in the ankle. Texas lore claims that General Santa Anna had requested his aides to secure an attractive and provocative young lady and bring her into the camp of the Mexican army the night before the battle, to entertain him. According to the legend, General Houston's army literally caught the Mexican General with his pants down. This rumor has never been reliably substantiated. What has been substantiated is the existence in the University of Texas Archives, the hand written lyrics to the well known and well loved song: "The Yellow Rose of Texas", purportedly written by a black musician, supposedly a former, (but escaped), slave from Louisiana. The lady who was the subject of the song was supposedly Emily West, a lovely mixed race freed slave who came to Texas from Connecticut as an indentured servant. She served as a housekeeper at a small hotel in San Antonio that was owned by her master. There is no reliable information as to whether or not Emily West was ever actually at San Jacinto, and if she was, how and why she was there. The rumor has been that she was a loyal Texan and was serving as a spy for the Texans. Again, this rumor has titillated untold thousands of people down through Texas history, but there has never been a shred of hard evidence to substantiate the story. The song was set to music many years later and a popular recording was made by band leader Mitch Miller.

The Mexicans were badly trounced and surrendered; a defeated and demoralized Army. Of the more than 1,500 men of the Mexican Army, 630 Mexican soldiers were killed and more than 700 surrendered. General Santa Anna discarded his General's medals and dress uniform and dressed as a common soldier, mingling with his enlisted men. He was discovered when one of his soldiers saluted him and addressed him as "El Presidente".

General Houston had no facilities in which to hold the Mexican prisoners, nor the ability to feed such large number of people. He agreed to release Santa Anna and his men and allow them to return to Mexico after requiring General Santa Anna, not only as the General of the Mexican Army, but as the President of the Republic of Mexico, to sign a formal surrender and an agreement to withdraw all Mexican troops from Texas soil and recognize Texas as a sovereign nation. For his actions, Houston was roundly criticized, by his army and by all of the government officials of the Republic of Texas. It was Houston's hope that the victory at San Jacinto and his release of Santa Anna and his aides would bring an end to the war and prevent additional bloodshed. His actions with his defeated foe were very similar to the actions taken by General Washington at the end of the Revolutionary War. Cornwallis and his army were released to return to England. For Sam Houston there were many battles ahead, militarily, as well as politically and psychologically. The victorious Battle at San Jacinto was won by the Texans on April 21, 1836. Texas was now a legitimate, full-fledged Republic, entitled to the respect and consideration of the other nations of the world.

Respecting the civilized rules of warfare, General Sam Houston had released General Santa Anna and General Cos, to return to Mexico after exacting their promise to not engage in any future hostilities with the

Texans. Remembering the Alamo and Goliad, the men of Houston's army were anxious to wreak their vengeance on the brutal enemy. In an effort to protect the lives of Santa Anna and General Cos General Houston had them smuggled aboard a ship in Galveston Harbor, bound for Vera Cruz. The ship was intercepted by a band of irate Texans before it sailed from the harbor. Santa Anna and a number of his men were held captive for several months by the Texans until General Houston and the Republic's government could convince the rebellious Texans to release them and a;;pw them to return to Mexico..

CHAPTER 18

A NEW REPUBLIC IS BORN

Following his victory over the Mexicans at San Jacinto, Sam Houston ran for President of the Republic in opposition to Stephen F. Austin and Henry Smith. He won in a landslide victory of 79% of the vote and served as President from October 22, 1836 until December 12, 1841. As President of the Republic, Houston demanded that Santa Anna and his men be released by their captors to return to Mexico in accordance with the surrender agreement. They were repatriated back to Mexico in 1837 on the orders of the President of the Republic of Texas.

Sam Houston's hospitality and respect for a vanquished foe would not be extended to Texas troops captured by Santa Anna in future battles between the Texans and the Mexican army. In future conflicts with the Texans, General Santa Anna would require the commanders of his troops to mutilate and put to the sword many captured Texas prisoners. His proclivity for the massacre and mutilation of prisoners became legendary. The battle cry of "Remember The Alamo" soon became famous for future generations of Texans and Americans alike.

The Republic of Texas was born with the victory over the Mexicans by General Sam Houston's army of Texans at San Jacinto. Following his defeat and before his return to Mexico, General Santa Anna had signed a treaty as the President of Mexico, ceding all of the territory north of the Rio Grande, including a part of the territory of New Mexico, Oklahoma, Colorado, Montana, and those parts of Texas that were included in the 1803 Louisiana Purchase, to the Republic of Texas. The Mexican Congress renounced the treaty, but under International Law, the Republic of Texas successfully claimed the ceded territory, which included the territory north of the Rio Grande, establishing the Rio Grande as the international boundary between Texas and Mexico.

Following the Texans' victory over the Mexicans, the next ten years was to be fraught with all but insurmountable problems for the fledgling Republic. Samuel Houston was elected the first President of the Republic of Texas on September 5, 1836. Now that there was an elected government in place at Velasco, and later at Washington on the Brazos, it had become a Republic but with no treasury, no money, no income, no system of law, no credit, no manufacturing industry of any kind, and hampered with an unofficial citizens army anxious to find an enemy they could do battle with. It was up to the leaders of this infant government and the individual citizens of Texas to bring some order out of the chaos to the loosely organized new Republic. It would require all of the patience, ingenuity, talents and efforts of the few men elected to office to hold together and develop the framework of a viable nation.

In the meantime, the Mexican Navy was supplying by sea the remaining Mexican troops still operating along the Texas Gulf Coast.. To prevent the supply and reinforcement of these hostile troops, it was imperative that quick action be taken at sea to halt the Mexican ships. Loyal private citizens quickly arranged for the purchase of a privateer ship named the "William Robbins" and rechristened it the "Liberty". Three other ships were later purchased, the "Independence", the "Brutus" and the "Invincible", all former American revenue ships that had recently been retired by the American Navy revenue collection service.. This gave the new Republic a small but formidable Navy. These four ships put to sea in the Gulf of Mexico, with captains and crews of inexperienced but dedicated Texans. They soon had complete control of the waters off the Texas Gulf Coast, attacking any ships flying the Mexican flag and seizing large amounts of valuable cargo. The few Mexican troops still left along the Gulf Coast soon high tailed it back to Mexico. Victory over the Mexican navy was a tremendous victory for the inexperienced "landlubber" sailors of the Texas Navy. Just one small indication of the patriotism and ingenuity of the Texans that would be repeated over and over again in the years to come.

When Texas declared its independence from Mexico on March 1, 1836, the first meeting of the provisional government of Texas met at Washington on the Brazos where David G. Burnet was elected interim President of the Republic to serve until a government could be formed and a permanent President elected. The newly formed government was in a state of uncertainty. Very little serious consideration apparently had been given to many of the practical decisions that would become immediate necessities when Texas became a sovereign nation. One pressing problem was where the seat of the new government would be. The unrest and the lack of information regarding the movements and the unknown strength of an approaching Mexican army converging on San Antonio and the Alamo caused President Burnet to move the government first to

Gonzales, then to Harrisburg, on the Buffalo Bayou, near Houston, as the temporary seat of the government. Following the Mexican victory at the Alamo, President Burnet and his cabinet boarded a steamboat, the Cayuga, at Harrisburg on March 15, 1836, resulting in the steamboat being the de-facto Capital of Texas. The President and his cabinet went ashore at Galveston, then journeyed to Velasco where the government remained until October. On October 22, 1836, General Sam Houston was elected President and he had the government moved again, this time to Columbia resulting in Columbia becoming the first declared Capital of Texas. Again, in December, 1836, he ordered the transfer of the government to the City of Houston.

The City of Houston served as the Capital until a Capital Commission was appointed and selected the town of "Waterloo" on the North bank of the Colorado River, a part of the original land grant given to Stephan F. Austin, as the site of the new Capital, and renamed the town "Austin" in honor of Stephen F. Austin. Austin was confirmed by the Texas Congress on January 19, 1839 as the permanent Capital of Texas. It was important to quickly establish a permanent facility for the seat of the government. The first Capital building of Texas was constructed of wooden planks.

Unfortunately, the Texans were not yet able to settle down with their government and to conduct its business. In March 1842, Mexican troops again captured San Antonio. President Houston once again ordered the government moved to Houston for its protection. All state officials, except President Houston, moved back to Washington on the Brazos rather than to Houston. They felt they had good reason not to return the government to the city of Houston. President Houston appeared intent on the City of Houston becoming the Capital of the Republic. President Houston sent a delegation to Austin to get the archives and take them to Houston. The Citizens of Austin were afraid that if the archives were moved to Houston, Austin would lose the State Capital permanently. In what was to become the "Archives War", the citizens of Austin rebelled and stopped President Houston's people from removing the archives. The Austin delegation was a determined group and Austin was once again declared to be the Capital of the Republic. President Houston had lost his battle to exercise his personal prerogative and over rule a majority of the government. It was important to quickly establish the authority of the elected government representatives. The government was of one mind and were not about to allow their wishes to be over ruled. The independent, brash, arrogant, perhaps uncivilized and ferociously independent, citizens of the infant Republic of Texas had spoken loud and clear that they would never again be dominated by or dictated to, by any one, not even one of their own

Protecting its citizens and securing its borders alone would have been a tremendous responsibility for any newly formed government and its army. But many other pressing responsibilities faced the fledgling nation. Just as a new born infant first learns to crawl and then to walk, the Texans, having learned the art of war, now began the learning process of peace and the art of sophisticated politics. Due to an existing agreement with Mexico, agreeing not to intrude into Mexican territory, and the Mexicans steadfastly continued to claim that Mexican Territory extended as far north as the Nueces river, rather than the Rio Grande. the United States was in no hurry to recognize the Republic, so the Texans had no choice but to conduct their political affairs accordingly.

Emissaries were sent abroad to secure recognition of the new Republic by other nations. In 1837, President Sam Houston dispatched J. Pinckney Henderson to Great Britain in an effort to gain recognition from the English of the new Republic and to negotiate a trade agreement. Henderson fell short in his efforts to secure recognition but succeeded in securing a favorable trade agreement with the English. Following Henderson's break-through with Great Britain on the trade agreement, several other nations suddenly became interested in the new Republic. First France, then the Netherlands, Belgium and finally Great Britain, extended recognition and signed treaties with the Republic of Texas. In the Plaza of St. James Courtyard in London,, on the entrance to the building across from St. James Club, there is still a plaque identifying it as the location of the Embassy of the Republic of Texas.

To understand the native personality and general philosophy of the Texan, one has only to be aware of the environment and the underlying conditions that created their individuality. Only men and women of great pride and determination could have so quickly organized a workable and dependable government for the Republic. They were unequivocally determined to be masters of their own future.

A vast majority of the settlers who came to Texas as pioneers, were a peaceful and God fearing, hard-working people, more than willing to live in peace and harmony with their neighbors. However, they were not about to be run rough shod over by any tyrannical government, Spanish, Mexican, American, or even their own government, as has been shown by their refusal to move the Capital from Austin back to Houston as President Sam Houston insisted. They were ever anxious to respond to a call to arms to protect their land, home, family, neighbor and their way of life. In times of necessity, local militias were formed to meet an emergency. Once the crisis was over, they were anxious to disband and return home to get on with their lives. The history of Texas is replete with records of such men. These early unofficial and unpaid militias, referred to as "ranging forces", called together for the mutual defense in times of crisis, were the forerunners of what was to later become the Texas Ranger Force. They were all volunteers.

The constant turmoil and internecine wars between the competing factions within the Government of Mexico, had the effect of limiting the size of the Mexican forces that crossed the Texas border. However, the frequent incursions nonetheless continued unabated. In March, 1842, six years after the Mexicans defeat at San Jacinto, Mexican troops under General Rafael Vasquez again over-ran a much smaller force of Texan citizen militia and recaptured San Antonio and the Alamo. General Vasquez and his troops stayed in the town only two days, then retreated south of the Rio Grande Such an excursion and violation of the Republic of Texas' sovereign7ty was not about to be tolerated. The Republic of Texas assigned Captain John C. Hays to be the leader of the militia forces. He was charged with the defense and protection of the Alamo and San Antonio and the area between the San Antonio River and the Rio

Grande. Hays was ordered to recruit 150 volunteers to serve in the militia, but the Republic was too poor to equip and pay even this small force of men. These citizen soldiers were, for the most part, farmers and family men. They were more than willing, and in most cases, eager, to serve in the militia during a crisis. But any lengthy service meant leaving their crops un-harvested, which would spell financial ruin, leave their families without food or provisions or any protection from marauding Indians during their absence.

In September 1842, Under the command of a German mercenary, General Adrian Woll, the Mexican army once again took San Antonio. Irate over another incursion of foreign forces into Texas, Captain Hays spread the word that San Antonio had again been taken by the Mexicans. Mad as hell, determined Texas citizens this time responded in large numbers. A leader of one of the small Texas forces wrote: "We fought all day until the enemy retreated, carrying off their dead. The enemy are all around me but I fear them not. I will hold my position until I hear from reinforcements. Come help me, it is the most favorable opportunity I have ever seen. There are eleven hundred of the enemy. I can whip them on my own ground without any help but I cannot take prisoners." Reinforcements arrived led by Captain Hays and, after a short but fierce battle, the Mexicans were routed and in full retreat. A few days later, the Mexican General Woll, offered a five hundred dollar reward for the head of Captain Hayes

Following the recapture of San Antonio by the Texans, Texas President Sam Houston ordered a detachment of irregulars, or citizen soldiers, to pursue the Mexicans across the Rio Grande in retaliation for their incursion into Texas. It was to be the most disastrous expedition ever undertaken by the Republic of Texas. Dubbed "The Mier Expedition," three hundred irregulars under the command of William Fisher attacked the Mexican village of Mier, just across the Rio

Grande, which was defended by a detachment of Mexican soldiers. Fisher was severely wounded during the desperate struggle. Without a strong leader, his men were soon overwhelmed. They surrendered to the Mexicans on the condition that they would be considered prisoners of war, treated humanely, and would be detained near the Texas border. Following their surrender, despite the promises of the Mexican officers, the men were marched into the interior of Mexico and held at the small pueblo of Salado, some fifty miles from the Rio Grande. There the Texans rebelled and seized their guards, along with their weapons and ammunition stores and took as their prisoners the rest of the Mexican infantry. Realizing that they had little chance of holding the Mexican prisoners once the Mexican army returned in force, they once again got assurances from the captured Mexicans that the Texan's wounded, if left behind, would be treated humanely as prisoners of war. Once they had the assurance of the Mexican officers, they released all of the Mexican soldiers and beat a hasty retreat in the direction of the Rio Grande, leaving their wounded in the care of the Mexicans. Being in strange territory, they were soon lost and out of provisions. They wandered aimlessly for several days without food or water in the hot, dry desert. In a matter of a few days they were recaptured by the Mexican army and taken back to the village of Saltillo, deep into the interior of Mexico. The Mexican President, General Santa Anna, the same man to whom General Sam Houston had shown the respect and hospitality of sparing his life, had returned to Mexico, and was again elected President. He decreed that all of the Texan prisoners, including the wounded, were to be shot. The American and British Ministers in Mexico City launched a vigorous protest and the order was amended so that only every tenth man was to die. A container was produced with one hundred fifty-nine white beans and seventeen black beans, equaling the number of captives. Each man was required to draw a bean from the container and the unlucky ones drawing a black bean were summarily shot. Texans never forgave Santa Ana for the manner in which he repaid the hospitality and humane treatment afforded him by General Sam Houston following the battle at San Jacinto. It was an act of barbarism that the Texans would never forget.

CHAPTER 19

ETHNICITY BECOMES IMPORTANT TO TEXAS

The early evolution of the Texans began with the immigration of a primarily English speaking people led by Anglo Saxons of English, Scottish and Scots-Irish descent. While there were other ethnic immigrants that came to Texas both before and soon following the revolution between Texas and Mexico, their numbers in comparison were very small. There would soon be various settlements of people of Germanic, Dutch, Polish, Moravian, French, Italian, Czechoslovakian, Spanish, and a smattering of many others of ethnic origins who migrated to Texas once it became reasonably safe to do so. Word soon spread of the vast expanses of land, forests, plains, mountains, sea shores, almost any type of terrain, flora and fauna found in various parts of Europe, were all available in Texas. As families of ethnic origins began to dribble into Texas, they were soon followed by other family members and friends from their mother countries. Soon the dribble turned into a steady flow of immigrants from all over Europe.

Throughout history, it has been natural of the human nature for people of like ethnic origins, language and customs to seek out others of the same cultural background. Many of the settlements that would later become towns and centers of trade and culture were formed during the early history of Texas. These settlements and towns were to contribute greatly to the culture, eclectic and ecumenical history of Texas and helped to establish the Texas culture and mystique that we know today. Many of those towns and centers of ethnic culture grew and prospered and are now well known.

Very early in the history of Texas, immigrants could sail directly from European ports into several small ports along the Gulf of Mexico. Many landed at Galveston and further south at Indianola. After the rigorous and often life threatening voyage across the ocean, the immigrants quickly found that the trials and hardships still facing them were even more arduous and difficult that they ever expected. They were faced with unexpected epidemics of malaria, typhoid and other diseases for which they were ill prepared. Usually there were no doctors available and no means of transport into the interior where medical treatment might be available. Many were stuck in unsanitary, temporary camps for weeks before they could arrange for oxen, mules, or horses to pull wagons or carts to transport them and their meager belongings into the interior. Nevertheless, many did survive and moved inland, especially up the numerous rivers empting into the Gulf of Mexico. The Brazos, Colorado, and Guadalupe Rivers sprouted established settlements and towns that later became centers of farming and commerce.

    The early settlers of Texas quickly learned to cope with the sparsely populated and wild country they found as they moved deeper and deeper into the unsettled interior. The original Texans had already established a code of ethics that was necessary to live in harmony with their neighbors. This code required that dealings and trade between one another be honest and trustworthy. To a great extent, most immigrants quickly adapted to these unwritten laws. Those found to be untrustworthy were very quickly found out and were excommunicated from the general society of Texans. A man's word had to be relied upon in order for commerce between the various areas of the state had to be conducted with trust and integrity. As the vast geographical areas of Texas grew, this culture became ingrained in most dealings of a business and societal nature. These unwritten rules of conduct carried forward in the transactions of business between the established citizens and later, between them and the new immigrants. There is little record of any organized or wide spread mistreatment of the new immigrants once they arrived on Texas soil.. This code of ethics has been a cornerstone of Texas culture ever since.

Once an immigrant family arrived at their chosen destination, neighbors were quick to pitch in and assist them in getting settled in their new homes. The new immigrants found forests that many were accustomed to in their mother-land. Further west they found the hill country and finally the mountains surrounded by the vast Texas plains. As they moved south they found the coastal plains and the Texas Gulf Coast. Texas was so vast that the geographic terrain that closely resembled the lands which they and their forefathers were accustomed to was easily available to them as they moved north, south and west.. A majority of the new immigrants found that farming, ranching and other agricultural related jobs were about the only occupations available. Before the land could be farmed it had to be cleared of trees, stumps and rocks for it to be tillable. Word quickly spread back to the home countries that land was plentiful and the climate was very similar to "home". As these new families began to immigrate to Texas from the French, Italian, Baltic, and other European countries, they soon established enclaves with their countrymen. Towns sprang up, essentially populated by people of the same ethnic, cultural and language backgrounds. These new settlers brought with them their unique cultures and way of life. Over time they greatly enriched the culture of the Texans and the Texas Wild West.

As the new settlers moved inland the route was uncharted and they had to travel cross-country, stopping for rest and supplies whenever and wherever they could find an established settlement where they could secure supplies to finish their journey. A majority of the early settlements were established at river crossings along the various primitive trails of migration. One way station on their trek inland was the settlement of Seguin, some one-hundred miles inland. The earliest history of the present town of Seguin, located on the Guadalupe River east of San Antonio, dates back some 10,000 years. First evidence of extended habitation of the location found by European explorers was the remains of a Tonkawa Indian settlement along the banks of the Guadalupe River. Later, Spanish, Mexican and Anglo settlers established farms and ranches in the area that was to become Seguin. The first recorded history of the area shows that Juan Antonio Navarro established a ranch there in 1831. The town of Seguin was founded on August 12, 1838, some sixteen months after Texas won its independence from Mexico at San Jacinto. The town was named for Juan Seguin, a veteran of the decisive battle between the Texans and Mexico at San Jacinto. Of Mexican origin, Seguin, a Texas patriot, was later elected a Senator of the Republic of Texas.

As the immigrants traveled north and westerly, they began to also establish settlements and towns along the way. A few of the more prominent of the settlements still existing today are San Marcos, New Braunfels and Fredericksburg. Settled almost exclusively by German and Austrian immigrants, the settlements quickly grew and became important centers of the Germanic culture. Unfortunately, a number of years later, after Texas had joined the American Union, this culture was to become a serious problem for the citizens of German descent at the outbreak of the war between the North and the South.

A majority of the citizens of German descent, especially at Fredericksburg, which was named for Prince Frederick of Prussia, were suspected of supporting the North in the conflict. Many of the German and Prussian immigrants, and their ancestors, had been vassals under the ruling class of Germany and Prussia. They had literally been indentured slaves. Their history led them to oppose slavery in any form. Few Texans owned slaves and most did not consider Texas to be a slave holding state. Some of the Texans sympathetic to the South, considered the German immigrants to be traitors to the Southern cause. Many of the German immigrants made their way to the northern states and fought for the Union. Others attempted to make their way to Mexico in an effort to escape the retribution of the Southerners. A few of them were captured by roving bands of hot headed "enforcers" before they could reach the Rio Grande and safety in Mexico. Unfortunately, some were summarily executed.

The distinct German culture is quickly obvious today to most visitors to the town of Fredericksburg. Many of the "old-timers" of German descent still speak primarily the German language and most teach their children the language. The typical German zeal for perfection in construction and the habit of building their homes and buildings of materials that will last for centuries is evident throughout the town, in their homes, barns and other structures on the farms and in the many stores and business structures in the city of

Fredericksburg. The popular German celebration of October-fest is very much alive, well and enjoyed. It is a festive time and, just as they did in the old country, the Polka is danced and German music played with vigor.

Originally, many of the farms were several miles from the center of their culture, schools and religion to be found in the town of Fredericksburg. The round trip from many of the farms to town and back was too far to travel by horse and buggy in one day. Many of the farmers built "Sunday Houses" in town and often the mother would stay in town with the children during the school term. In the summer when there was no school, the entire family would load up and travel into town and spend the weekend in town where they could visit with their friends and neighbors. Fredericksburg is dotted with many of these relatively small, quaint and extremely well built Sunday Houses. Most of the houses are now owned by local town citizens as their residences. These new immigrants greatly influenced the Texas culture through their hard work and industry, their frugality and ethical business practices.

The town of Schulenburg was founded in 1842 and was named for Louis Schulenburg, one of the original settlers. The town still has a large population of German, Austrian, Czechoslovakian, Polish and Jewish descent. Schulenburg bakeries are noted among other things, for their kolaches, a pastry greatly enjoyed by the Czechs, Poles and Moravians.

There are dozens of such towns spread by the new immigrants all over Texas. In most of them, their native culture is still evident.

CHAPTER 20

CAPTAINS RICHARD KING AND MIFFLIN KENEDY

In 1847, during the Mexican War, River Boat Captain Richard King moved to the Rio Grande in deep South Texas where he joined his friend, Captain Mifflin Kenedy. Together they commanded a river boat, the Colonel Cross for the U. S. Army for the duration of the war. It was to be a life changing move for both men and would have a huge influence on the history of Texas and the aura of the Texans. After the war, Kenedy formed the M. Kenedy Steamboat Firm and with King formed the King, Kenedy Company. These two Steamboat firms were to dominate the river trade on the Rio Grande for more than twenty years.

Richard King was born in New York City, the son of poor Irish immigrants. At the age of nine he was indentured to a Manhattan jeweler. Within a very few years he ran away and stowed-away on a ship destined to

Mobile Alabama. En route he was discovered and put to work as a cabin boy for Captain Monroe. When the ship reached Mobile, Captain Monroe, along with a friend, Captain Holland, took young Richard under their wing and schooled the boy in the art of navigation. For the next six years he worked aboard steamboats plying the Alabama rivers. During this time he had eight months of formal schooling in Connecticut, courtesy of Captain Holland. He had earned his ship pilot's license by the age of sixteen. In 1842 he enlisted in the army for the duration of the Seminole war in Florida, where he met Captain Mifflin Kenedy, who became his mentor and life-long friend.

Captain Kenedy learned of the need of the U. S. Army for steam boats to navigate the Rio Grande River on the border between Texas and Mexico. With Captain King, he sailed his steam boat along the coast of lower Texas to Brownsville, where both Captains contracted to haul army supplies north up the Rio Grande as far as they could operate their steam boat. During the years of his activities as an Owner/Captain of steamboats plying the dangerous Rio Grande, Captain Kenedy and Captain King soon began to reveal their expertise as hard-nosed business-men. Captain King also proved his talent as an innovator. He constructed boats that were capable of navigating the treacherous and fickle Rio Grande. His motto was that he could take a boat "anywhere a dry creek flows".

In addition to his river boat business, Captain King soon had his fingers in several different business adventures with different associates. In the early 1850's he began speculating in undeveloped South Texas land. At one point he invested in a Spanish land grant for a large majority of South Padre Island. It was soon proven that the land grant was bogus and worthless. Captain King learned his lesson well. Thereafter he purchased land through his lawyers, James Wells and Robert Kleberg, from Corpus Christi, both of whom would figure prominently not only in his future but the future of Texas as well. From 1853 to the time of his death, he had purchased and taken title to more than 614,000 acres of ranch land in south Texas. This was the nucleus of the famed King Ranch.

During the "War Between The States ", Richard King and Mifflin Kenedy joined forces and entered into several contracts with the Confederate government to license their river boats under the Mexican flag and exsport cotton through the small Mexican port of Baghdad. The resulting cash flow allowed the Confederacy to purchase munitions and supplies needed to sustain the Confederate Government in its pursuit of the war.

Following the war, Captains King and Kenedy were both accused of being Confederate sympathizers and threatened with severe punishment by the American government. Both men quickly moved across the border to Matamoras, Mexico. They lived in Mexico for three years until they could secure a pardon from American President Andrew Jackson. King and Kenedy dissolved their partnership in 1868 and went forward as individual businessmen. King kept the Santa Gertrudis portion of the King Ranch and Kenedy kept the Las Laureles division, becoming the two most famous ranches in America. After Kings death in 1885, his lawyer Robert Kleberg soon married King's daughter Henrietta, and took over management of the huge ranch.

Richard King and Mifflin Kenedy had a tremendous influence on the cattle industry and ultimately on the future of Texas . Their business ventures helped develop a great swath of South Texas. Even today to thousands of people both in America and countries in many parts of the world, just the name of the famous King Ranch evokes visions of cattle, cowboys, Indians and bandit battles to people around most of the civilized world. They truly helped mold Texas and the Texans.

CHAPTER 21

THE TEXAS RANGERS

All of the experiences that the Texans have encountered during their many trials and tribulations, have had a great influence on the character and personality of the Texans. There is one organization that, more than any other, has placed an indelible stamp on the Texans. The name of the Texas Rangers has become synonymous with law and order in Texas. Their exploits have fascinated people from around the world along with generations of Texans. Hundred of books have been written and movies have been made depicting their exploits. The lore and the reputation of the Rangers is a legacy that helps to define who Texans are. The Texas Rangers are a part of Texas' legacy like no other group of individuals.

The fledgling government of the Republic realized that in order to protect its citizens, maintain the domesticate peace and to protect its borders against future foreign incursions, it was an absolute necessity to recruit and equip, to the best of their ability, a force of state militia. A small core of recruits was already available among the citizens who were already defending the citizens against marauding Indians and Mexican violators of the border and had shown their desire and ability to enforce the peace. This citizens militia was already referred to as Rangers, although the name of the organization was not yet official.

In 1838 Mirabeau Bonaparte Lamar was elected President of the Republic of Texas. He was an able and aggressive President. He was determined to stop the murderous forays by the Indians and incursions by the Mexicans. Early in his presidency, the state legislature, with Lamar's encouragement, passed a law establishing several companies of mounted volunteers to be called

"Rangers" for the protection of the frontier against the Indians. Thus was born the official Texas Rangers force that would play a large role in the history of Texas and on the character of future Texans.

The Rangers furnished their own horses, saddles, firearms, clothing and any personal items needed for their survival. The Republic provided provisions, horse shoes and medicines in an amount not to exceed $10.00 per man per month. This small, unique force of men served more through a feeling of patriotism than the small monetary stipend they were paid. They established a reputation unequaled in American history. They were famed for being able to ride like an Indian, shoot like a Kentuckian, think like a Mexican and fight like the Devil. The adage of "One riot, one Ranger" is a part of Texas Ranger lore. In those instances where only one Ranger showed up to quell disturbances, it was most generally a situation where only one Ranger was available at the time. In many areas of Texas there was no organized civil law enforcement. There were no jails or places in which to confine miscreants. Most often the Rangers had to define their own law, frequently administering the law to meet the circumstances. They asked no quarter and, if the offense was serious enough to warrant, they gave no quarter and the perpetrator was either shot or hanged on the spot. The reputation of the Texas Ranger was respected as no other law enforcement organization in history. A mere rumor that the Rangers were on their way was often sufficient for the lawless to head for other parts of the country rather than await Ranger Justice.

While most of the newly organized Rangers were occupied with fighting to protect the Mexican border, the absence of able-bodied men and the lack of any organized defenses, allowed the marauding Indians to be free to kill, rape and take captive, women and children along the entire northern and western frontier. There were many incidents of heroism in the annals of the Rangers. One such incident occurred in January, 1838.

During the night a young woman, the wife of a settler, stumbled into the camp of a company of Rangers bivouacked some thirty miles north of present day Austin. Along with her husband, brother and two small children, they had been traveling by wagon to their home on the Guadalupe River when they were attacked by a band of Comanche warriors. Her husband and brother were killed. She, along with her two small children, were taken captive. One of the children, a baby girl, cried continuously from terror, and the mother, being tied to the back of one of the wagon mules, was unable to comfort the child to prevent her crying. The Indians, tiring of hearing the child scream and in order to hush the child they bashed her head against a tree, killing her instantly. The mother escaped during the night and slipped away from the Indian camp and wandered for hours, finally and only by accident, she stumbled upon the Ranger encampment and alerted them to the plight of her small son, still a captive of the Comanche. By riding swiftly for several hours, the Rangers located the Indian camp and immediately attacked. One Indian was killed and the rest escaped. The small boy was rescued and returned to his mother.

One of the most famous stories of the Indians capture of an Anglo child is that of Cynthia Ann Parker. In 1833 at the age of eight Cynthia Ann moved from Crawford County, Illinois to Texas with her grandfather, John Parker, the son of a nationally famous Patriot and soldier. He had been recruited by several Texans to establish a fort in North Central Texas as a protection for the settlers against Indian raids. Parker built a log fortification, later to be called "Fort Parker", for his family and the families of several neighbors near the Navasota River in what is now Limestone County. On May 19, 1836, a force of over 100 Indians, made up of Comanche, Kiowa and Kichai warriors attacked the fortification and quickly overwhelmed the outnumbered settlers. The warriors took Cynthia Ann, her grandfather and several others alive. The horrified captives were forced to watch as the women were raped and the men were tortured and killed. The last to be killed was John Parker. He was scalped, castrated and his genitals stuffed into his mouth before he was finally killed.

Cynthia Ann remained with the Comanche tribe for almost twenty-five years. Finally, in 1860, she was found by the Rangers and returned to her family. During her life with the Comanche, she had become assimilated into the tribe and could not adapt and return to the old life of her Anglo people. Extremely depressed over the separation from her two children, she refused to eat for long periods. Physically debilitated from lack of nourishment, she caught influenza and died in 1870 at the age of 40 years. Upon reaching maturity, her son, Quanah Parker was chosen to be Chief of the Comanche and wrecked havoc among the Anglo settlers for many years before he was captured and returned to the reservation in Oklahoma. He later became a model citizen and assisted in quelling hostility between his Comanche tribe and the Anglos.

Volumes have been written and countless movies made about the Texas Rangers and their exploits in the taming of the wild and rugged land of Texas. Most of these accounts depict the Rangers as swashbuckling, fast-riding, invincible heroes, always at the ready with their deadly six guns. The truth is considerably different. The "six shooter" revolver wasn't invented until long after the Rangers had become a household name. Their primary weapon was the rifle, loaded with powder, primer and ball. This rifle could not be reloaded on horse-back. The rider had to dismount in order to fire a second, and perhaps if he was lucky, in rare instances, a third shot. The Mexican foe was similarly handicapped and therefore an equal opponent. The Indian on the other hand, was equipped with the bow and arrow, the lance, and his ever present knife and tomahawk. Unless the Indian could be repelled in the initial attack, the

Texans were in an inferior position since the Indian warriors could shoot their arrows from horseback while at a full gallop. This was especially true when the settler was attacked in his homestead. The settler might have two or more rifles loaded and at the ready, but when the shot from these loaded weapons was exhausted, he had little left with which to defend himself and his family . With the invention of the "six-shooter", or Colt revolving pistol, the tide was turned.

In 1836, a sailor, named Samuel H. Colt, first invented the notorious six-shooter that only a few years later was made famous on the Texas frontier by the Texas Rangers. It was originally designed so that it had to be broken apart in three pieces in order to be loaded after the first six shots had been fired. When the hammer was cocked and ready to shoot, a concealed trigger dropped down. Since it had no trigger guard, it was susceptible to being accidentally fired. Although Samuel Colt was unable to find a ready market with the U.S.

Army, in some manner, a few of the new revolvers found their way to Texas and into the hands of the Texas Rangers. This new revolver was a huge improvement over the unwieldy rifle but as constructed, could not be reloaded on horseback. The Republic of Texas sent Ranger Samuel Walker to New York to purchase arms on behalf of the Republic. Samuel Walker spent several days with Samuel Colt suggesting modifications to the revolver. The new weapon was redesigned with a fixed trigger, a trigger guard, and the revolving chamber redesigned so that it could be reloaded on horse-back without dismantling. This new weapon, the Colt 44, was named the "Walker Colt" and gave the Texas Rangers a distinct advantage over their foes, including Indian, Mexican and renegade American desperadoes. The six-shooter, along with the Spencer Rifle and later the Winchester Repeating Rifle, were the preferred weapons of the Texas Rangers. The Rifle, the long range weapon and the Walker Colt a short range pistol, were to become the Texan's best defense against their foes.

CHAPTER 22

THE ANNEXATION OF TEXAS

The American government did not formally recognize the Republic of Texas until March 3, 1847. A resolution was reluctantly passed by the American Congress and signed by President Andrew Jackson on that date and the Republic of Texas was finally recognized as a sovereign nation by the United States. Several bills were presented over the next several years to Congress calling for the annexation of Texas but were tabled, claiming that annexation would violate a United States treaty with Mexico, promising that the United States would not recognize any foreign nation between the borders of Mexico and the United States.

Suddenly the idea of an independent, sovereign Texas nation, with lands stretching from the Gulf of Mexico on the South to the present state of Wyoming on the North, effectively blocking the westward advance of the American dream, was worrisome and even intolerable to the American government. The American Congress belatedly began to realize the extent of their folly in not extending statehood to Texas.

Recognition of the Republic of Texas by foreign powers meant that the Texans now had serious bargaining power with the American Congress. Instead of a mere territory appealing for assistance and protection, the American Congress was now negotiating with a sovereign Nation. A Nation that had to be brought into the fold of statehood at any cost or else revise or abandon the dream of an American nation extending from sea to sea. The annexation of all previous states had been on terms dictated by the American Congress. The terms for the annexation of Texas would be on terms, if not dictated by, at least favorable to the Texans. Among other concessions Texas, was to retain state ownership of all public lands, and the right to divide into four separate states if the Texas legislature decided to do so. The American Congress now eagerly voted for annexation and on December 29, 1845, President Polk signed the act that merged Texas into the American Union.

Texas is the only State over which six sovereign flags have flown. It has been governed by five different sovereign nations. It had its own constitution, flag, (The Lone Star), militia, navy, statewide law enforcement and diplomatic representatives in several foreign nations. It is the only State that upon it's admission to the Union was granted the right to divide itself into four separate states if its citizens should so desire. Upon joining the Union, the government of the Republic of Texas was wise enough to retain solely to the State of Texas, all of the public lands lying within its borders, the only State allowed by the Union to do so. Texans were extremely fortunate to have wise, patriotic leadership in the earliest days. Texas and Texans would not have survived for very long otherwise. Texans have endured many struggles and each struggle has influenced the character and personality of the Texans.

The annexation of Texas into the Union touched off the U.S.-Mexican war in 1846. Two battles between U.S. and Mexican troops were fought near Brownsville at Palo Alto and Resaca de la Palma. Prior to the annexation of Texas, the Mexicans had claimed the Nueces River as their border with Texas. The treaty between General Houston and Mexican General Santa Anna, established the border as the Rio Grande. The Mexican government refused to honor the treaty, but the Texans continued to claim the Rio Grande as the border under International Law. It wasn't until 1846, after Texas had agreed to join the Union, that the ultimate border between Mexico and Texas was to be formally recognized by the American government as the Rio Grande. In July 1846, a few months before the formal annexation of Texas was to occur, the American government sent General Zachary Taylor with a small army to Corpus Christi, a few miles north of the Nueces River, to await the formal annexation due to transpire on December 31, 1846.

Following Texas' annexation, General Taylor immediately moved his troops to the area of the Rio Grande near Brownsville in order to establish once and for all the border between the United States and Mexico. The Mexican government protested the move, claiming that the boundary was still a matter of negotiation. When General Taylor refused to leave the area of the Rio Grande, the Mexicans declared war on the United States on April 24, 1846.

In March, 1847, U. S. Army General Winfield Scott, landed his army at Vera Cruz, Mexico and soon marched into Mexico City and ended the war between the U. S. and Mexico. The Capture of Mexico City brought about the Treaty of Guadalupe Hidalgo which permanently established the Rio Grande as the boundary between Mexico and the United States. The war was officially ended on February 2, 1848.

Near the end of the U. S.– Mexican war, Mexican President, General Santa Anna, along with his wife and members of his family, was once again captured near the pueblo of Jalapa deep in Mexico by General Scott's troops. Following his capture and after considerable negotiations, General Santa Anna was released and issued a safe conduct pass to Mexico City for himself, his wife and family and his military advisors, on the order of the U. S. Commanding General of the American army, General Winfield Scott.

A company of Texas Rangers, serving with the U. S. Army as scouts, was camped nearby. Upon hearing that General Santa Anna had been released and he and his family had been given safe conduct along with his contingent of Mexican army guards, several of the Rangers, irate over having lost relatives or loved ones massacred at the Alamo or Goliad, were intent upon killing Santa Anna. Texas Ranger Captain John Hays was determined to prevent the murder. Realizing that revenge for the massacres was ruling the men's passions, Captain Hays appealed to the men, not as an officer, but as a man and a fellow Texan. He pointed out that Santa Anna had been condemned by the world for his cruelty and butchery; a stain upon his reputation as a man, as President of Mexico and as a soldier. He was a prisoner of war within his own country, and was traveling with a safe conduct pass issued by the United States Army's Commanding General. For the Texans to murder him would be an act the civilized world would brand as an assassination and a blot on the reputation and history of Texas. Captain Hays then asked: "Would you so dishonor Texas?" The Rangers replied: "Then we will not do it." They allowed the open carriage bearing Santa Anna, his wife, daughter and his guards to pass unmolested. Full of grief and anger, the Rangers still refused to dishonor themselves and their beloved State of Texas.

When the war ended, and upon the signing of the Treaty of Guadalupe, all U. S. troops were withdrawn from Mexico. The end of the war brought peace between the United States and Mexico, but did not end the conflict between Texas and the Mexicans. Raids against Texas ranchers by Mexican banditos from across the Rio Grande were a regular occurrence. Skirmishes and "mini-wars" back and forth across the Rio Grande continued well into the twentieth century.

CHAPTER 23

WAR AND PEACE

During the 1850's, a massive effort was made to round up hostile Indians and confine them to reservations in Texas. A treaty was signed by the chiefs of a large number of the Comanche tribes, agreeing to lay down their arms and remain on the reservations.

Frequent raids by renegade Comanche warriors continued and many settlers blamed the raids on the reservation Indians. A Texas Ranger company under the command of Captain John S. "Rip" Ford (or Rest In Peace, a nick name given Ford for his deadly aim), was called in to investigate the raids. Captain Ford found that a few of his men, angry over the atrocities committed against innocent and defenseless settlers, were determined to fasten guilt on the reservation Indians regardless of the facts. He learned that there would be an attempt to fabricate evidence pointing to the reservation. Ford declared: "That will not work. I am responsible to the State and to public opinion, and I will take no step in the matter unless I am backed by facts of such a character as to justify me before the public. I am willing to punish the Comanche if they are guilty, but I am not disposed to do so unjustly and improperly." It was an honorable decision made by an honorable man under extreme circumstances. The conspiracy fell apart. Many such acts of valor by the Texas Rangers are threaded throughout the history of Texas. Following Ford's decision and on the recommendation of the Texas government, the United States government closed the reservations in Texas and moved the Indians to reservations in Oklahoma Territory.

Bandits from both sides of the Rio Grande were stealing herds of cattle and horses and driving them across the river into Mexican territory before the army could arrive. It was a lucrative business for the bandits, for they had a ready market for beef and horses with the Spanish army in Cuba. The stolen livestock were being shipped by sea from the small Mexican port at Bagdad, just across the Rio Grande south of Brownsville. Although the U.S. Army had established a Fort at Brownsville, the American Government prohibited the army from crossing the Rio Grande into Mexico to pursue the bandits.

The annals of history are replete with stories of the darker side of mankind. There have been and always will be, those who sulk just beyond the pale of the law, waiting for the opportunity to prey on honest men and women, the weak and the defenseless. As the frontiers of America moved south and westward, these scavengers tagged along, not to contribute to society, but to seek their prey wherever they could find it. The new frontier of Texas attracted its share of those scavengers, many of whom frequented the border on the Rio Grande. The vastness of the territory, the remoteness and lack of sufficient federal military troops, placed an almost overwhelming burden on the Texans. The major responsibility of security for the citizens and enforcement of the law fell on the small force of the Texas Rangers. The Rangers were ordinary men with little, if any, formal military or law enforcement training. The Captains of the Ranger troops were generally men who were capable of leading their men in battle against the marauding Indians and, in a few cases had served in the U.S. – Mexican war as scouts. They were ordinary men called upon to perform extraordinary service in extraordinary times. The greater majority of these men proved themselves to be equal to the task. It was often their responsibility to weed out the miscreants and misfits wherever they found them, even among their own ranks.

While Texans were being menaced by hostile Indians in north and west Texas, the ranches and farms along the Rio Grande were being plundered and settlers were being killed by bands of thieves from across the Rio Grande. These bandits were both Mexicans and Indians, but included some Anglo desperadoes, seeking refuge in Mexico. The Mexican army had no desire to intervene on behalf of the Texans. A large number of the affected settlers and ranchers were Mexican by birth but had settled in Texas and were now Texas citizens. The U.S. Army constructed forts along the Rio Grande in an effort to cope with these raids by Mexican bandits. The vastness and remoteness of the territory made it impossible for the regular Army to provide protection to the ranchers and farmers, leaving that responsibility to the self-created bands of armed citizens, often referred to as "vigilantes". Unfortunately, a number of outlaws and other unsavory characters took advantage of the opportunity to form their own clandestine gangs to steal and plunder, primarily targeting ranches and farms owned by citizens of Mexican descent. These bands of outlaws committed numerous atrocities against the local Mexican landowners, plundering and burning their ranches and farms, either killing or driving them from their homesteads. The situation became so bad there was a real fear of civil war breaking out between the Anglos and the Mexicans

In 1861, Texas Ranger Captain L. E. McNelly and a company of Rangers was dispatched to the area with instructions to settle the disputes and to seek out and bring to justice those responsible for the outrages. Using his well-established reputation and authority as a Captain of the Rangers, McNelly ordered the vigilantes to disband, and told the local, well meaning citizens to take their weapons and go home. There being no jails in the vicinity in which to hold the outlaws, he told the interlopers to be gone and not return, else they would be shot on the spot.

Not being fluent in Spanish, Captain McNelly enlisted the aid of a number of the Mexican ranchers to supplement his force and interpret for him if and when he could capture the bandits who were well armed and had a plentiful supply of fresh horses. With their ability to cross the border into Mexico almost at will, it was important to locate and surprise them before they could make a run for the border. The bandits ravaged the border, killing ranchers and homesteaders indiscriminately, both Mexican and Anglo alike, stealing their cattle and horses and terrorizing those within their reach. The U.S. army had little success in pursuing the bandits due to their standing orders not to cross the Rio Grande. The bandits, took their sanctuary in Mexico, pillaging and burning from the mouth of the Rio Grande west to Laredo and as far north as Corpus Christi. It was a daunting task for one Ranger Captain.

Soon Ranger Captain Rip Ford was dispatched to South Texas to work with Captain Mc Nelly in breaking up the bandit gangs. Captain Ford left Austin with only eight men, little food and no money. On his way south, with typical Ranger ingenuity and resourcefulness, he was able to recruit and deputize additional men, secure contributions of wagons for transport and enough money to tide them over until they could reach Brownsville. He arrived in Brownsville with more than fifty hardened and experienced fighting men. Ford and his Rangers, supported by a small contingent of soldiers from the Army barracks at Fort Brown swept west along the Rio Grande in hot pursuit of more than three hundred bandits. Although greatly out-numbered, the Rangers, in spite of their tired men and horses, with superior marksmanship and bravery, put the gang to flight, leaving more than sixty of the renegades either dead or dying.

The skirmishes of Captain Ford and, his troop of Rangers along the border, soon established a reputation that has become a true part of Texas lore. Once on the trail of bandits and cattle rustlers, the Rio Grande posed no barrier to the Rangers. Unlike the Army, the Rangers became adept at pursuing bandits across the Rio Grande into Mexican sovereign territory, killing some and scattering the rest, in order to retrieve the stolen herds of cattle and returning them to their rightful owners. Mexican outlaws soon learned that to tangle with "Los Diablos," as they called the Texas Rangers, meant serious injury or instant death. Through their fearless exploits, Texas Rangers earned respect from outlaws, renegades and banditos alike.

CHAPTER 24

WAR CLOUDS ARE RISING

Events between the southern states, including Texas on one hand and the north on the other, were about to erupt into a war between the North and the South that would change America, Texas, the Texas Rangers, and all Texans for many years to come. Some scars still remain.

In the election of 1860, sufficient signatures were not obtained to place Abraham Lincoln on the Texas ballot, so, while not popular in the state, Lincoln was not eligible for election in Texas. The population of Texas had almost tripled in the ten years between 1850 and 1860. The first census data for the state was compiled in 1850, following annexation, the population was 223,380. In ten years, by 1860, the population had grown to 604,215, a growth of 270%. A majority of the new settlers were from the southern states of Louisiana, Mississippi, Alabama and Georgia. Prior to 1850, slave ownership in Texas was virtually unknown. Many of the new immigrants from the South were slave owners and they had a large influence in the secession of Texas from the Union leading to the outbreak of the War between the States. A convention was called by the legislature to meet in Austin to vote on secession from the Union. Only twenty-five percent of those attending the convention to vote had been in Texas during the early days of the Republic, prior to annexation. There were very few slave owners in Texas and slavery was not of any great concern to those original Texans. The other seventy-five percent of the voters were relatively new immigrants from the old South and had a far greater interest in slavery. The result of the vote for secession was 71percent for and 29 percent against. The lop-sided vote was an accurate reflection of the sentiment of those that were representative of the original settlers of the Republic of Texas who did not wish to secede from the Union, nor to join the South in their squabble with the North.

Sam Houston, as the elected Governor of Texas, refused to recognize the legality of Texas' secession from the Union and refused to take the oath to be loyal to the Confederacy. He was evicted from the Governor's office by the secessionists majority in the legislature on March 16, 1861. He continued to defend Texas but refused to accept it's secession from the Union.

CHAPTER 25

WAR BETWEEN THE STATES

For more than 150 years there has been a disagreement between the people of the "Southern " states and those from the "Northern" states about the root causes of the war between the North and the South. Many Southerners refer to it as "The War Between the States", refusing to call it the Civil War. The matter has never been researched for the differences between "The War Between the States" and "The Civil War". Many older Texans just called it "The War", without distinguishing "which" war, just assuming that everyone knew which war they were referring to.

(Curious as to the reasons for this anomaly, I studied the history of the War between the North and the South. I discovered that there very well could be some validity in the differences of opinion. Following is a synopsis of what I have found in my research of the matter.)

In the mid 1800's there was great economic disparity between the country's northern and southern states. In the North, the economy was primarily based on manufacturing and industry. Any agriculture in the North was limited to small family farms and gardens. The economy in the South was based solely on agriculture; a system of large scale plantation farming, primarily of cotton and tobacco. These crops were very labor intensive, with most of the labor being done by black slaves. Transportation of their commodities was by railroad. The few railroads that existed in the south were owned by rich industrial tycoons living in the eastern states. Freight rates in the South,(below the Mason-Dixon Line) were much higher than comparable commodities and distances by rail in the north. The exorbitant freight rates were ruinous to the southern economy. Southerners had battled for several years in an effort to get the freight rates equalized with those in the north. As a result, export of these commodities to

England and other European countries represented a majority of the economy of the Southern States. There was a growing sentiment in the North against slavery, especially the extension of slavery into the newly opened Western Territories. This led many southerners to fear that the continuance of slavery in the southern states was in danger. The sudden abolition of slavery in the southern plantation states would have devastated their already struggling economy.

There was animosity between the "Northern Faction" in Congress and the "Southern Faction" who were adamant about States' Rights. The northern block feared the voting strength of the somewhat larger southern block of legislators who were referred to as " States Righters". There were considerable differences between the attitudes, both political and economic, of the North and the South. In 1854, the U. S. Congress passed the Kansas-Nebraska Act, essentially opening the new territories to slavery. Pro and anti slavery sentiment led to violent confrontations in Kansas, earning it the nick-name of "Bleeding Kansas". In 1857 the U. S. Supreme Court ruled in the Dred Scott case, that slavery was legal in the new territories. In 1861 tensions between the North and South exploded over states' rights versus Federal authority. The abolitionist ,John Brown's raid at Harper's Ferry in 1859, and the northern states coalition's support of the raid, had convinced the southerners that states' rights and legal slavery, although ruled constitutional by the United States Supreme Court, would soon be ignored by the Federal Government. In 1861, the election of Abraham Lincoln, feared to be strongly against states' rights and against slavery, was the final straw. His election led to the secession of seven southern states. Four more joined them after the first shots of the war were fired.

Initially, slavery in the southern states was not an issue. In view of the Supreme Court ruling, the southern states were primarily concerned with states' rights and the fear that those rights were about to be usurped by the Federal Government. It was only after hostilities had raged for almost two years that the slavery issue in the South was introduced by President Lincoln and became such an emotional issue that it later eclipsed all other factors that had lead up to the secession of the southern states and to the outbreak of the war between the states. In President Lincoln's inaugural address, he stated very clearly that he had no wish to interfere with slavery where it already existed. Even in the early months of the war, President Lincoln several times unequivocally stated that he was fighting to "save the Union, not to free the slaves". On September 22, 1862, President Lincoln, in an effort to coerce the Southerners, totally contrary to his previous promises, issued a threat to the Southern Confederacy that "If the seceded states do not lay down their arms and return to the Union by January 1, 1863, I will declare their slaves forever free". When the date came without capitulation of the Confederacy, he issued his famous Emancipation Proclamation freeing the slaves. The Southern States never accepted the premise that the war was a "Civil War" or that slavery was the issue that caused the hostilities. The Southern States contended that the war was a conflict between the States because of the Northern States' stand on States' Rights. To a great many Texans the reference to "The War", still means "The War Between the States".

CHAPTER 26

TEXAS JOINS THE CONFEDERACY

Texans are not prone to divide their loyalty. Once the decision was made to secede from the Union and join the Confederacy, most Texans, with some trepidation, were steadfast in their support of the Southern cause. In the case of Texas' secession from the Union, unlike the other southern states, under the terms of Texas' annexation with the Union, Texas retained the right to secede from the Union by a simple popular vote, and further, could divide its territory into separate states if it's citizens so desired. Technically, the Union had no right to even be in Texas after the war unless Texas should again agree to annexation.

Thousands of Texans marched to the North to join the confederate forces in Louisiana, Mississippi, Alabama and Tennessee. The small minority that refused to join the confederate cause quickly made their escape across the border to Mexico. When Union troops finally appeared in south Texas in an effort to blockade the port at Brownsville, a few of the renegades joined the Union army. A majority of the soldiers stationed at Fort Brown were colored, or "Buffalo Soldiers" as they were referred to, and at the end of the War, were to be the focus of many problems between the citizens of Brownsville and the soldiers garrisoned at Fort Brown.

Other than Brownsville on the Mexican border, the only major port in Texas on the Gulf Coast was at Galveston Island. There was a smaller port at Sabine Pass at the mouth of the Sabine River, but it could not accommodate deep draft ships. In September, 1862, the Union navy blockaded the ports along the Gulf Coast from Florida to Texas, including Galveston, and Sabine Pass effectively stifling the export of cotton, the only viable commodity produced in the South that was attractive to foreign nations. Without the revenue from the export of cotton, the South could not purchase the arms and supplies necessary to prosecute the war.

Fortunately for Texas and the South, England and France were heavy importers of cotton. In January, 1862, Confederate General John B. Magruder retook Galveston for the Confederacy, using two steamboats lined with cotton bales protecting sharp shooters with devastating results to the Union forces. Three weeks later Magruder used two more steam boats lined with cotton bales and sharp shooters to retake the port at Sabine Pass. Late in 1863. The Union navy launched a major offensive against the Texas Gulf Ports with better success. Sabine Pass and Galveston were effectively blockaded along with the port at Brazos Santiago, then five days later took Brownsville and its Confederate Army headquarters. Colonel John S. "Rip" Ford, by now given a commission in the Confederate army, rushed to South Texas with Texas State troops and routed the Union Army at Brownsville in July 1864. While Brownsville was back in Confederate hands, the port at Brazos Santiago, near the mouth of the Rio Grande was again available to shipments to

European countries with cotton from Arkansas, Louisiana, and the cotton-producing areas of Texas, and they soon began shipping their cotton by wagon train to South Texas for export at Brownsville, then through the mouth of the Rio Grande at Brazos de Santiago by river steamers, called lighters, where it was trans-loaded onto French and British ships in deep water. Recognizing the small gap in their blockade, the Union soon sent troops to occupy Brownsville to seal the gap. Texas Ranger Colonel Rip Ford again quickly assembled a small Army at San Antonio of some six hundred or more old men and boys, too old or too young respectively, to serve in the regular army. Without supplies and forced to live off the land, they proceeded in a 250 mile forced march south to Brownsville. The Union army met them within a few miles of Brownsville. After seeing the size of Colonel Fords force, the Union army, having no stomach for real battle, promptly discovered their error and turned back to Fort Brown. With the aid of Texans who had fled across the Rio Grande to Matamoros, Mexico, to escape the Union troops, Ford and his irregular troops soon confronted the Union army at Fort Brown at Brownsville. The Union troops again made a hasty retreat, this time to Brazos Island at the mouth of the Rio Grande where additional Union troops were garrisoned. Now in control of Brownsville, Ford convinced Captain Richard King and Captain Mifflin Kennedy, the famous ranchers and river boat captains, to transfer their steamboats to Mexican registration. Now flying the Mexican flag, they resumed the export of cotton through their small "port" at Baghdad, Mexico, to the foreign ships waiting off shore. The Union Army could only stand helplessly by on Brazos Island as the steamers, flying the Mexican flag, plied back and forth with their cargo. There was a steady stream of wagon trains hauling bales of cotton all across south Texas destined to Brownsville and the foreign ships waiting off shore. The ability to export cotton and import supplies through

Baghdad and Brownsville earned the Confederacy the cash for supplies, and arms to prosecute the War that were otherwise unavailable, all of which was critical to sustaining their cause.

The Confederacy was well served by the loyalty and ingenuity of Texas and Texans on all fronts during the War between the States. More than ninety percent of the able bodied men of age in Texas volunteered for service to the Confederate cause. More than sixty percent of those were either killed or wounded. Most survivors had no money, no possessions, no mode of transport, and frequently were severely wounded. Many never made it back to Texas and to their homes. Wives, children, mothers and fathers and other family members often never knew what happened to their loved ones.

Due to distance and the lack of telegraph communications in the remote areas of South Texas, word that General Robert E. Lee had surrendered the Confederate army at Appomattox on April 9, 1865, did not reach either the Confederate troops or the Union troops at Brownsville until May 14, 1865, weeks after the war ended in the rest of the country. The last battle of the war was fought at Palmito Hill near Brownsville more than a month after General Lee had surrendered his Army of the Confederacy. The Texans, led by Colonel "Rip" Ford, whose force was out numbered as usual, routed the Union troops, many of whom were southern renegades, sending them fleeing for their lives across the Laguna Madre to Brazos Island and the Union encampment, leaving more than 200 dead and wounded out of the original 300 Union troops.

CHAPTER 27

RECONSTRUCTION AND MARTIAL LAW

Texas, like other Southern States, suffered terribly during reconstruction. After the war, carpetbaggers and politically appointed hacks from northern states flooded into Texas. They came to seek any possible personal gain from their conquered foe, generally arriving with the few belongings they owned in a carpetbag, hence the term "Carpetbaggers". The Texans had suffered a bitter defeat. Texas had lost more than a quarter of its able-bodied men in battle and what little economy had existed before the war was now destroyed. Defeat in war, ignoble though it was, the Texans could understand and accept, but the humiliation and outrages that were heaped upon the state and the people by the revenge hungry Yankees after the war, was beyond the tolerance of the Texans. The great majority of Texans had never owned slaves nor had they trafficked in slavery, so there was no real opposition to the abolition of slavery. Texas' secession from the Union was less in support of slavery, than it was in sympathy with the South in their conflict with the Northern States over states rights.

During the war, slave owners in Arkansas, Alabama, Louisiana and Mississippi, had shipped more than one hundred thousand of their slaves to Texas in an effort to keep them out of the hands of the Union Armies. These poor souls were now free, but they had no place to go. Homeless and jobless, they now had no choice but to roam the towns and countryside in search of food and shelter. Under martial law, the Union army, in obvious retaliation and revenge for Texas secession from the Union, removed all former state and local law enforcement personnel and all elected officials from office. What local officials were appointed by both the civilian and military leadership most often had no experience in civic operations or leadership nor the duties that were to be performed. A majority of them were uneducated and uninformed as to their duties and their authority. Most often they were political "hacks", appointed through friendship or, in some cases, were family relatives of other Union appointees.

Without any law enforcement, chaos reigned. The proud and independent Texans felt there was no reason, or any cause for the total subjugation of Texas by the Union after the war ended. Texans had carved their land out of the wilderness, fought the Indians and the Mexicans with aid from no one, and had won the right to live in peace and manage their affairs without outside interference. In some instances, Union troops, led by inexperienced, egotistical Union officers bent on revenge, marched through the countryside pillaging and terrorizing the citizens, and in several instances, burning entire towns. Notably, the Union troops avoided the frontier where they would encounter hostile Indians, but confined their presence to the relatively safe, inhabited areas. In those rare cases where any remaining civil authority was not divested of their authority and job, they were prohibited from arresting, charging, or incarcerating any freed slave or Union soldier for any reason whatsoever. Total anarchy reigned for months after the end of the war; the Union Army officers were either refusing or unable to restore order. When the war was over, Confederate money was worthless, leaving the citizens in dire circumstances with no money and no way to earn money to buy necessities or support themselves and their families. Few people had money of any value with which to pay for work or services, so employment was all but non-existent . The Union army bought a majority of their food and supplies locally, but the army set the value and in most cases paid the Texans only a fraction of the worth. The Texans could not complain or demand fair payment, because there was no official agency to whom they could complain or ask for redress. To the proud, independent and stubborn Texans, such treatment was intolerable. The State was under strict

Union Army martial law for nine long, insufferable years. It was an era that fostered a seething rage and distrust of Federal intervention into State affairs. The determination never to bow to conquerors again would be indelibly stamped in the character and personality of native Texans.

The years following the end of the War between the states, from 1865 to 1874, were the blackest and most devastating period in Texas history. When Texas seceded from the Union, it was the newest state in the Union. Texans were still in an all out war with the Indians and fighting almost daily skirmishes with the Mexicans along the Rio Grande from Brownsville to El Paso. Before the war, the U.S. Army had stationed several contingents of troops along the frontier and the border, but they were singularly ineffective in subduing either the Indians or the Mexicans. The state government was still in its infancy and only just beginning to cope with the needs of its citizens.

Under orders of General Tecumseh Sherman, a new state constitution was drafted in 1869 calling for the election of a new state government. With the state under total military rule, the commander of the Union Army in Texas appointed the registrars to register the voters. Any citizen who had served with the Confederacy was prohibited from voting. Most of the former slaves and voters allowed under martial law, were uneducated and were ushered to the polls in droves and allowed to cast their ballots without the necessity of even registering. The fraudulent and unconstitutional election of 1869 elected E. J. Davis Governor. The Texans presented the U S President and Congress with irrefutable evidence of the wholesale fraud but were unconscionably ignored. Davis immediately formed a State Police force with unlimited power. Using the State Police as a political tool of repression, he issued badges to political friends, and criminals. The State Police force created by Davis came to be the most hated organization in Texas history.

During the period of reconstruction, the historical records of Texas are rife with documented incidents of political repression, oppression of citizens, murder, theft, embezzlement,   fraud and corruption, theft of state and public funds, abuse by carpet baggers, and the usurpation of the civil rights of Texas citizens.

One example of the extent of the outrages of Texans occurred on May 18, 1871. A wagon train led by a Mr. Henry Warren, was traveling between Jacksboro and Belknap Road near Fort Worth when it was ambushed by a group of Kiowa and Comanche warriors. The travelers immediately circled their wagons, placing the teams of mules in the center of the circle. After a hard fought battle, the Indians killed and then mutilated seven of the twelve travelers. Luckily, five men managed to escape. Governor Davis ignored the massacre, refusing to send troops or the State Police Force in pursuit of the Indians. Several months later, three prominent Indian chiefs were arrested near Fort Sill, Oklahoma Territory, after they had bragged about their involvement in the massacre. General Tecumseh Sherman happened to be visiting the army base. He ordered the three chiefs to be delivered back to Jacksboro, Texas near the site of the massacre, to stand trial. On the way to Jacksboro, Chief Satank tried to escape and was shot and killed. The other two Indian chiefs were tried and convicted. Chief Santank and Chief Big Tree, according to court records of the sentencing of the convicted murderers, were sentenced by Judge Soward to "Hang, hang, hang, until you are dead and may God have mercy on your soul". Governor Davis quickly commuted their sentences to life in Prison at the State Prison in Huntsville, Texas. For what-ever reason that history does not record, both Indian chiefs were released from prison on parole in 1873 after serving less than two years for the murders.

CHAPTER 28

TEXANS STRIVE TO RETURN TO NORMALCY

Life in Texas had never been easy. It became ever more difficult following the War, with so many of Texas' able bodied men killed during the war. In addition, any semblance of state government had been eradicated. Law and order were practically nonexistent. Each family and community had to look after their own and try to keep peace with one another. Some of the Union Army Forts had contingents of good, honorable men. Others were poorly staffed with inexperienced officers and wild, raw recruits and miss-fits. Many of the immigrants had built their homes as near as possible to the existing Forts for protection from the Indians. At some of the Forts, when forays were ventured forth by the Army, the men and their officers were inexperienced and most often fled and had no luck in quelling the Indian raids on the settlers.

The next Gubernatorial election was in 1873. The Texans had had enough of military occupation, imposed government, and carpetbaggers. Texans took over the polls, and proceeded to elect their own slate of government officials by hook or crook. Known carpetbaggers were told by armed men to stay away from the polling places. Men, women, young boys, criminals, thieves, anyone with a warm body and who was loyal to the State of Texas was ushered to the polls to vote for the Texans. Richard Coke was elected Governor by a margin of two to one. The Texans had learned well, a lesson in the arrt of power politics.

Following the election of 1873, reconstruction Governor E. J. Davis claimed fraud and presented the case to the Davis-appointed Texas Supreme Court. The Court ruled in favor of Davis, declaring the election unconstitutional, fraudulent, and invalid. Remembering their experiences of just a few years earlier, the Texans were unwilling to accept the biased ruling of the State Supreme Court and having won the election by an overwhelming majority, the Texans refused to be intimated. Once again, they were determined not to be run rough shod over by politicians they considered to be illegitimately serving in positions of power. The new Governor and newly elected state legislature ignored the Supreme Court ruling, were sworn in and proceeded to conduct the State's business. One of the first orders of business was to abolish the State Police force formed by reconstruction governor Davis and replace them with Texas Rangers. By a law that was enacted by the legislature, there can never again be a State Police Force. Now, more than one hundred-twenty five years later, the primary statewide law enforcement organization is known as the Texas State Highway Patrol, or more commonly, the State Troopers. The Texas Rangers continue to be a statewide criminal law enforcement and investigative agency operating under the direct supervision of the Governor.

Through perseverance, stubborn dedication to their cause and unflinching determination to restore

Texas to its rightful independence and freedom from outside rule, the fourteenth legislature began the healing process. A constitutional convention was called in 1875 to rewrite the state constitution. The duly elected delegation was composed primarily of older, pre-war Texans, and included farmers and lawyers, Democrats, Republicans, white men and black men. The delegates wrote a new State Constitution and the fundamental laws for the state of Texas that have endured for more than a hundred years.

Following the adoption of the new constitution and lacking a viable economic base, the legislature explored every avenue available to find ways to cut spending, including salaries at every level of government. The salaries of government officials were slashed. The number of offices reduced. The number of judgeships reduced and made into elective offices rather than appointed positions. The legislature also declared railroads to be common carriers subject to state regulation, giving Texans the right to control freight rates within the state.

While the number of elective offices was reduced and many state positions around the state were eliminated, the state government in Austin had necessarily grown along with the population. The space in the old state Capital building had become totally inadequate for the legislature and other necessary offices to effectively operate. Unwilling to incur any further debt, the legislature decided to sell sufficient state owned land to finance the construction of a new state Capital building. The original Capital was a primitive building, constructed of cedar planks. It had served its purpose but a much larger building was desperately needed. In the largest barter arrangement to take place in the world at that time, the legislature of the State of Texas passed a constitutional amendment allowing the state to sell to a conglomerate of investors from England, 3.000,000 acres of state land in the Texas Panhandle for sufficient money to build a new State Capital. This is the land that became the huge XIT Ranch, the largest cattle ranch in the world and the deal financed the building of the largest building under one roof in the world.

During the War between the States, the economy had been destroyed in the South. The U. S. Congress returned the nation to the gold standard in 1879. Immediately, the currency was de-valued by more than 30%. As a result, the agricultural economy in the South collapsed. Between 1880 and 1890 the number of farms in Texas doubled but the number of tenant farmer tripled. Many of the farmers had lost their farms and had become tenant farmers. The eastern railroad monopoly completely controlled the railroads and interstate freight rates. Shipments moving between points within Texas, (Intra-state), were controlled by the Texas legislature. Shipping rates on cotton and other farm products and on cattle more than tripled making the shipment of commodities to the northern and eastern markets prohibitive.

In 1890, James S. Hogg was elected Governor. Hogg was not allied with either of the political parties and owed no favors to any block of politicians. Following his election the Texas legislature created the Railroad Commission and gave it control of all common carriers, effectively ending the railroads' control of freight rates. Governor Hogg was elected to a second term by a very small plurality.

The backbone of the Texas economy was the cotton farmer. A majority of the shipments of cotton and other trade was through the port of Galveston. The entry of the Texas and Pacific, (T&P), and the Missouri-Kansas-Texas, (Katy) and the Southern Pacific railroads into Texas drastically changed the patterns of freight shipment in the state. Cotton and oil suddenly began to be shipped by rail rather than through the port of

Galveston where it was loaded aboard ships destined to the east coast and Atlantic ports.

The railroad owners secretly entered into an agreement to stop competitive rail track construction and share the tracks where possible, and to purchase any competing railroads in the state. Although the Texas legislature had enacted laws governing transportation and freight rates, eastern railroad investors effectively prevented any effective regulation through the threat of withdrawing their capital investments from Texas. The monopoly of the railroads brought the Texas economy to its knees and all but stopped all economic expansion. It was evident to the citizens of Texas that the elected legislature was unresponsive to their needs and that a crisis was at hand. In the election of 1890, only 22 of the 106 sitting legislators were returned to Austin. A hopeful attitude of change was sweeping the state. The Texas Railroad Commission was created by the Texas legislature in 1890, with authority to regulate the transportation of all freight in Intra-state commerce, (between points within the state) by rail, pipeline or motor vehicle. Its authority would also soon be expanded to include the oil industry by regulating the amount of production at the well head.

CHAPTER 29

ETHNIC IMMIGRANTS BEGIN TO DEVELOP TEXAS

It has often been said that people are molded and shaped by the influence of the time, the place and the experiences in their life as they grew to adulthood. Their persona is reflected by the genes of their ancestry and the influence of their experiences. These factors are well inscribed in a vast majority of native Texans. The time, place and their experiences are what have made Texans different.

Strong and courageous leadership was required for Texas to be developed and to ultimately become viable and a successful society and economy that it has become. Those leaders left their personal mark not only on the State, but on the people who were their neighbors, partners, employers. employees, and friends and that relationship is what ultimately molded and shaped them into Texans. A vast majority of those leaders came to Texas as pioneers and were themselves molded and shaped by their experiences, hard work and toil that made them the leaders they were to become. Space and time allows for the mention of only a few of those leaders.

Early in this narrative, it was mentioned that descendents of the original Reynolds family migrated to Texas from Alabama in 1847. One of those descendents, Barber Watkins Reynolds, his wife, Anne Marie (nee Campbell), and others of his family, decided to stake their future on a life in this new frontier, called Texas. It was a momentous decision. At that time Texas was a wild and undisciplined land of desperadoes, lawlessness, uncivilized Indians and other unknown trials and tribulations. Of her and her families' arduous migration into this unknown wilderness, Sallie Reynolds Mathews, daughter of Barber Watkins Reynolds and his wife, Anne Marie, wrote in her chronicle "Interwoven, A Pioneer Chronicle". the reflection that: "in this conglomerate mass of humanity, there was also a leaven of good. Those rugged, self disciplined pioneers, men and women of fore sight and courage, who were willing to brave the dangerous unknown and undergo countless hardships and privations for the sake of widening their horizons and preparing an easier road for their children and those to come after them."

Mr. Reynolds first traveled to Texas alone to scout the country in Shelby County, in East Texas. After locating and purchasing acreage for cotton farming in Shelby country. He sent for his wife and their two children, George Thomas, aged three and William David, aged one. From Wetumpka, Alabama They took a river boat on the Coosa River, then on the Alabama River to Mobile Bay, then up the Mississippi River to New Orleans. They took another boat up the Mississippi to the Red River, then up the Red River to Shreveport, Louisiana. At Shreveport, Mrs. Reynolds hired a team of horses and a driver for the inland trek to East Texas. On their way, when night caught them, if there was no farm house nearby, they camped in the wilderness. At some point during their journey from Shreveport, her husband met them on the trail and accompanied them the rest of the way to their new home. After twelve years spent farming cotton in East Texas, the decision was made to move further west to West Texas which was recommended by a traveler who had been there with the words: "West Texas is fine country for men and dogs, but hell for women and horses". Not a very encouraging recommendation for pioneers heading into the vast territory and Indian infested country known as The Llano Estacado, or "Staked Plains" in English..

Upon their arrival at their new home in Throckmorton County, near present day Albany,, they discovered the country side in an uproar over the killing of a young man by hostile Indians. Their first experience with the west Texas frontier was seeing the formation of a posse and the chase out into the wilderness by a group of dedicated men intent on catching the perpetrators.

The posse was successful and returned with several Indian scalps. Not a very pretty sight, but proof that the culprits had been apprehended.

Not all of the new Texas settlers were honorable. In one instance a group of Indians were in the area near Old Fort Davis and they killed a prominent young man of the community. A posse of men was quickly formed and went in pursuit of Indians, just "any Indians" that they might come upon. The men were so riled up that evidence of guilt of the killing mattered not. They came upon a lone Indian brave doing nothing more threatening but roasting a skunk for his meal. The men ordered the Indian to march away from them. He did so and they shot him in the back killing him on the spot. No one ever knew if that particular Indian Had anything to do with the murder of the white boy or if he was even a member of the party that did the killing.

Buffalo were so numerous in the area of Old Fort Davis, that they infringed on the various ranches, destroying the grass the ranchers depended on for their cattle. Ranchers killed so many buffalo that they began to keep only the tongues for meat and the forelock from the head to use in the making of mattresses and pillows. There was no timber or trees from which lumber or building materials could be made. The hides were scraped and dried, then worked with tallow to soften them and used for making shirts and pants. They were not pleasant to sensitive noses, but were very serviceable on the frontier. On the plains, most early houses, or more accurately, hovels, were made of partially dug out depressions on hillsides, covered with brush and the front was made of small tree trunks or logs with the gaps between covered with a mixture of wattle and mud for the roof, covered with squares of sod. These shelters were very uncomfortable and leaked when it rained. Fortunately, West Texas is a semi arid country and rains were infrequent. These dugouts offered little protection from marauding Indians.

The area often selected for their home was many mile from civilization. Water was very scarce but a necessary commodity. When a flowing river or stream is nearby, the houses had to be built quite a distance away to avoid the danger of flooding during the rainy season. This made it necessary for water for any purpose to be carried a long distance in buckets. A wearisome and back-breaking chore.

The nearest post office was more than a hundred miles away and accessible only by wagon or horseback. Neighbors, living many miles apart, would being what mail there was for their nearest friends whenever they made the trip to town. There were no churches, preachers or Sunday School for the children. But there were plenty of Indian raids stealing livestock, especially horses, and frequently killing the settlers and their families. It was a hard and demanding life for the settlers, but their attitude was: "here we are and here we stay". The Indians were no respecters of human life.

When the Indians killed a settler, the men would mount up and make every effort to catch up with the marauders and take what revenge they could. In most instances, by the time the men were gathered and set out on the Indians trail, it was far too late to accomplish anything.

In 1854, a roving band of Kickapoo Indians killed a Colonel Stem, who had formerly been an Indian Agent for the area. He had retired and bought a farm and ranch in Throckmorton County. The commanding officer at Fort Arbuckle, sent word to the Kickapoo chiefs, telling them that he had information and proof that the murder had been committed by their people and demanding that the guilty person or persons be immediately turned over to his command. An intensive search was launched over a wide area. The Kickapoo chiefs confirmed that two of their people had committed the crime and promised that when they could apprehend them they would turn them in. Shortly afterward, one of the guilty braves was caught. He was firmly bound and placed on his horse to be taken to the Fort. The brave managed to free himself and threw himself from the horse in an effort to escape. He was immediately caught and shot. His dead body was delivered to the Fort. The other fugitive managed to escape detection and managed to elude capture. After several days, tired and hungry, he made his way to his brother's lodge in the nearby village. He confessed the murder and confirmed that he was the other man involved. He was fed in his brother's lodge and after satisfying his hunger, his brother took him a ways from the village and told him: "Brother, you have disgraced our tribe and it is my duty to kill you. For all of your life I have counseled you that your actions could one day lead you to this end. It will be painful for me, but it is my duty to see that justice is done". Stepping behind his brother he split his head with a tomahawk and then repeatedly struck him to make sure he was truly dead. A council was called and the brother told the council what he had done, noting that he knew it was his duty to kill his guilty brother. He asked that the body be beheaded and taken to the Fort, since the weather was too hot to preserve the body. He asked for volunteers to do the deed and to take the body to the Fort. There were no volunteers so he did the deed by himself and carried the head to Fort Arbuckle and delivered it to the Commander of the Fort. It was a barbaric method of justice, but it was the code of his tribe.

The property originally purchased by Colonel Stem in 1850 and was ultimately to become the property of Barber Watkins Reynolds. The original patent was issued by the Republic of Texas to Thomas Lambshead, an immigrant from Devon, England in 1848. It has remained in the Reynolds, (and later the Mathews family after the marriage of Sallie Ann Reynolds to John Alexander Matthews), as the Lambshead Ranch until today. The ranch at one time consisted of more than 50,000 acres of land. The ranch sets along the old Butterfield stage and Pony Express route which operated from 1857 until its demise, but the route was kept open for travelers and migrants moving west for many more years. The Lambshead Ranch is well known today for its history of continuing the century old tradition of the annual Fandango celebration begun by Sallie Reynolds Matthews' father almost a century ago.

CHAPTER 30

GOODNIGHT-LOVING CATTLE TRAIL

Brothers of Sallie Ann (Reynolds) Mathews, eventually migrated to far west Texas and established the "Long X" ranch and the Reynolds cattle Company. In 1868, one of the brothers, "Will", gathered a small herd of cattle and was joined by Charles Goodnight and Oliver Loving, (pioneers of the Goodnight-Loving cattle trail to Santa Fe, New Mexico and on into Colorado). With the large herd now complete, the three friends, along with their cowboys, began the long trek to Colorado. After having crossed the Pecos River from Texas into New Mexico, Mr. Loving decided to move ahead of the herd and go to Fort Sumner, New Mexico. He was accompanied by a young man with only one arm. Several miles from the herd, near the Pecos River, the two men were attacked by Indians. Mr. Loving was wounded and both men had lost their horses to the Indians. The two men concealed themselves under a rock outcropping on the banks of the River where they remained for several days, afraid to come out as there were still several Indians searching for them. Unable to walk, Mr. Loving sent the young man back in an effort to find the herd and secure their help. Lacking food for several days and no water after leaving the river, the young man became too tired and dehydrated to continue. He lay down in the meager shade of a Spanish Dagger, a form of yucca, with long dagger-like leaves, near where he was sure the herd would pass. He was found by his brother, one of the cattle drovers, and was given food and water. After resting a bit the young man led a rescue party to where Mr. Loving lay hidden. Loving was taken to Fort Sumner where he was put in the Fort's hospital. Unfortunately, he had become badly infected and without antibiotics, he soon died from the infection. A sad fate for one of Texas' original pioneer cattle men and explorer. This true saga was the subject and material for the popular movie, "Lonesome Dove".

The Reynolds brothers partnered with Charles Goodnight, on several drives from Throckmorton County and from their ranch near Fort Davis, to Colorado and Wyoming during the Colorado Gold Rush in the 1800's. Charles Goodnight was a pioneer cattleman responsible for the improvement of beef cattle by breeding the Durham bull to the Longhorn/Hereford blood line with the resulting off-spring that endured the long cattle drives and produced more and better beef.. He established his massive ranch in the Palo Duro Canyon in the midst of the huge area of the "Llano Estacado", (meaning Staked Plains). The Llano Estacado escarpment is an area of some 32,000 square miles of barren tablelands in west Texas that was all but impenetrable due to marauding Indians. Charles Goodnight struck a deal with the Comanche to furnish them free, one beef per month to feed their tribe. Goodnight established a friendly, live and let live accommodation with Quanah Parker, Chief of the

Comanche Indians. They were to become life-long friends.

It was in the Palo Duro Canyon that the U.S. Army, under the command of Colonel Ranald Slidell McKenzie, located the Comanche Indian Tribe, led by the famous Comanche Chief, Quanah Parker, (the son of the young Cynthia Ann Parker who was taken captive by the Comanche some twenty years earlier). Col. McKenzie escorted the Indian tribe back to Indian Territory in Oklahoma. After his capture, Chief Quanah Parker made peace with the U.S. and agreed to keep his tribe on the reservation and cease raiding and pillaging west Texas. With the capture of the Comanche Chief, and his influence over his large tribe, the Indian wars on the Texas Plains considerably diminished, making west Texas relatively safe from Indian attack for settlers and cattlemen.

CHAPTER 31

A "BLOWOUT" SHAKES TEXAS

Since its birth as a Republic, then a State, the Texas economy was almost solely an agricultural economy. That scenario was about to change. An unprecedented change in the history of Texas came on January 10, 1901 with the discovery of a massive reservoir of oil at Beaumont when a wild cat oil well nicknamed "Spindletop", burst through the Texas soil to become the largest oil gusher in history at that time. Almost overnight Texas was thrust into the industrial age. The State of Texas would never be the same. Oil production and industry would soon out strip agriculture as the economic engine that drives Texas. Texas was literally blown into the 20th century. Before it could be capped, Spindletop blew more than 100,000 barrels of oil per day 150 feet into the Texas sky for 9 days. It was the first oil field developed along the Texas Gulf Coast.

Fortunately for Texas and the oil industry, the Texas Railroad Commission had caused strict anti-trust laws to be passed by the Texas legislature prior to the development of Spindletop. Standard Oil Company had dominated the oil industry in Pennsylvania and along the east coast, preventing private companies from the opportunity to develop. Although Standard Oil developed numerous refineries in Texas, the states' strict anti-trust laws prevented the company from dominating the industry. Several new companies, such as Texaco and Gulf Oil sprang up and became the dominate oil producers in Texas. Within less than a year, the economy in Texas had changed from agriculture to oil related enterprises. Houston was quickly to become the headquarters location for many of the major oil, gas, and related businesses in the world. It would soon become the largest oil and oil products deep water port in the world.

"*A MAJOR DISASTER* STRIKES *THE TEXAS GULF COAST*", was the headline for all major newspapers around the world. The greatest single disaster in Texas history struck at Galveston on September 8, 1900 when a massive hurricane all but obliterated the city, killing an estimated 6,000 people. The survivors literally "pulled themselves up by their bootstraps" and rebuilt their city and their economy. There were no provisions for state or federal disaster aid. It was up to the citizens to rebuild their lives, homes and businesses on their own. In typical Texas fashion, they immediately rolled up their sleeves and began the rebuilding process. As they rebuilt their city, they also formed the first Commissioner form of government, a system of government that was to later become popular in many cities throughout the United States.

One of the tragedies for Galveston that its citizens could not prevent nor overcome, was the loss of a large majority of the port traffic through the Galveston Port to the inland water way port of Houston. The hurricane of 1900 reinforced proposals by Houstonians to build an inland waterway that would be protected from such natural disasters in the future. The devastation in Galveston caused the closing of the port there for many weeks, with the loss of shipping that was never regained. A deep water channel was dug from the Gulf of Mexico some 20 miles up the lower course of the San Jacinto River to the Buffalo Bayou where a massive port was built. The Port of Houston would quickly grow to become the largest port in the United States and the sixth largest in the world. More petro-chemical, crude and refined oil and fuels and thousands of other products move through the huge port than any other port in the world. The advent of shipping by closed containers loaded aboard ships constructed especially for that purpose, quickly doubled the traffic through the Houston Port.

CHAPTER 32

RANGERS GET THIER MAN

Some of the first men not native to Texas to qualify for Texas Honorary Citizenship, (at least in native Texan's minds), and thereby be entitled to all of the rights native born Texans enjoyed, including "bragging" rights, were Texas Rangers. One such outstanding Ranger was John B. Armstrong. He was born in Tennessee but moved to Texas when he was twenty-one years old. His most famous exploit was his capture of the infamous outlaw and the most renowned "gun slinger" in the West was, John Wesley Hardin. Hardin was wanted by the Texas Rangers for the killing of a Comanche County Deputy Sheriff. Though still recuperating from a gunshot wound received in the line of duty, Armstrong asked for permission to go after Hardin.

Discovering that Hardin was no longer in Texas, but hiding out in Alabama, Armstrong got a search warrant, went down to Alabama to arrest and return him for trial. By the time Armstrong arrived in Alabama, Hardin and four members of his gang had moved on to Florida. Armstrong tracked them down in Florida. Learning that the outlaws were on their way to Pensacola by train, Armstrong entered the front of the coach. Although hampered by his wound and the necessity to use a cane, he drew his Colt 45 and confronted Hardin and his gang. One of the gang drew his pistol and shot at Armstrong who returned fire, killing the man. By a fluke, Hardin's pistol got hung up in his suspenders allowing Armstrong time to swat Hardin over the head with his pistol rather than shooting and killing him. He disarmed the other three men and returned all four to Comanche County Texas for trial. Hardin was convicted and sentenced to twenty-five years in the state penitentiary at Huntsville.

Hardin wrote his autobiography, then studied law while in prison and was pardoned in 1894. He went to El

Paso to testify for the defense in a murder case and decided to stay and practice law in El Paso.

Unfortunately, he let his law practice flounder while he carried on an affair with the wife of one of his clients. Hardin conspired with several law enforcement officials to kill the husband of his paramour. Unfortunately one of the conspirators in the affair, Constable John Selman, shot and killed John Wesley Hardin instead. So ended the saga of at least one Texas desperado. John B. Armstrong retired and acquired and established a large and a very successful cattle ranch in Kenedy County, Texas adjoining the King Ranch. One of his grandsons was to become the President and General Manager of the huge King Ranch until his death. His other grandson, Tobin Armstrong, operated the Armstrong Ranch for many years until his death. Armstrong descendants still own and operate the ranch, (located near Kingsville, Texas.)

CHAPTER 33

TEXAS RANCHES AND RANCHERS

Texas is well known for its large ranches. Early in Texas history, there were many such ranches in Texas. One of the few remaining ranches still in the ownership of the original family is the McAllen Ranch, located west of present day Edinburg. John McAllen was the son of Irish immigrants. He migrated to south Texas near the Rio Grande in the mid 1800's. John soon married Salome Balli Young, the widow of John Young and, the daughter of a wealthy Mexican merchant who was the beneficiary of a large land grant, the Santa Anita grant, from the king of Spain. The original grant was made to Don Jose Gomez, a wealthy merchant of Reynosa, Mexico, located across the Rio Grande from present day McAllen. At that time the town was known as "Nuestra Senora de Guadalupe de Reynosa, established in 1759". Don Gomez took possession of the land, consisting of fifteen square Leagues, (4,428 acres per league, a total of approximately 66,475 total acres of land), in 1790. The award of the proposed grant was confirmed in 1790, and was given through an Initiation Ceremony of Possession by a representative of the King of Spain, Chief Justice Jose Francisco Balli Villareal. The ceremony consisted of a rite of possession by the Chief Justice taking the hand of the grantee and, both hands uncovered, proclaimed:"in the name of his Majesty, the King of Spain, whom may God protect, I put Don Manuel Gomez in possession of said land and as a sign of right of property to them, the said Gomez pulled out grass, broke sticks, threw stones, sprinkled water and made all of the other demonstration of the true possession, made many and gave repeated thanks to his Majesty, the King of Spain for the gift he has made him". Chief Justice Jose Balli Villareal was the brother-in-law of Don Manuel Gomez who was later also awarded Porciones, (portions), 63, 64 and 65 along the Rio Grande. The

Porciones were smaller tracts of land that fronted the river and each porcione had access to the river and its water. These parcels of land, along with the huge Santa Anita grant, were later inherited by his daughter Salome. The town of Hidalgo was built on one of these parcels. Salome married John Young, a business man from Reynosa and the three parcels of land that Salome inherited were soon joined with the Santa Anita grant. After the death of her husband, Salome married John McAllen. It was the beginning of what was to become the McAllen Ranch.

John McAllen and his wife Salome prospered as land developers and merchants on the border with Mexico. John Mc Allen gained prominence not only as a land developer and rancher, but was elected County Judge of Hidalgo county and later as a state representative from his district.

During the war between the states, the McAllen Ranch entered into agreements with both the Union and the Confederacy to furnish beef to their respective troops, through Fort Brown at Brownsville. During the period following the war, the ranch made several cattle drives of large herds over the Chisholm trail to Dodge City, Kansas. The operation of the ranch required more than 200 workers and vaqueros. Armed and mounted bandits from across the Rio Grande frequently raided the ranches north of the Rio Grande, necessitating armed guards to patrol the fences of the ranch to protect not only the cattle but the workers and residents of the ranch. There were numerous raids and several lives were lost.

In 1892, the ranch consisting of more than 50,000 acres, was split into two divisions, the Santa Anita and the San Juanito, with John and Salome retaining the operation of the Santa Anita and their son John Balli McAllen assuming responsibility of the San Juanito division. Salome Balli McAllen died in 1908 and John McAllen passed away very soon after, in 1913. The ranch experienced several difficult years following the death of John McAllen. After a few years, their nineteen year old son took over the ranch and very soon made the ranch once again productive. Bandit raids were still a frequent problem. In 1915 a very serious raid was staged on the San Juanito division, involving a large gang of bandits, armed and mounted, who attacked the ranch house. Mr. McAllen was at the ranch alone except for the lady housekeeper. The raid lasted several hours, with the housekeeper reloading the guns and John running from window to window, keeping the bandits at bay. More than five hundred rounds of ammunition were fired during the raid. Evidence of the ferocity of the raid is evident by the bullet holes still evident in the walls of the ranch house. The raid was so unnerving to Mr. McAllen that he moved into the town of McAllen, named for his father. Subsequently, he refused to go to the ranch unless he was armed and accompanied by armed guards.

Upon the death of his father in 1913, James B. McAllen's son, Argyle McAllen assumed the management of the ranch until his death, when it fell to his son, James B. McAllen. Jr.. Over the years the ranch has had good times and bad, but each time it persevered and bounced back, still intact and is still raising cattle and improving the herds each year under the management of John B. McAllen, Jr. The McAllen Clan has made a substantial contribution to the history of Texas. It is hoped that they will keep the ranch intact for the foreseeable future. The McAllens were and are true Texans, shaped and molded by the Texas frontier and the frontier life.

Don, (a courtesy Spanish title), Francisco Yturria was a very astute business man in both Mexico and Texas. He was born in Mexico prior to the revolution of Texas and the victory at San Jacinto that created the new Republic of Texas. While Don Francisco was a successful businessman he amassed an even larger fortune during the American war between the states. He joined

Captains Richard King and Mifflin Kenedy in assisting the Confederacy in exporting cotton through the small Mexican port of Baghdad. Through Don Francisco, the partnership of King and Kenedy licensed their river steam boats in Mexico and were able to circumvent the Union blockade of the Texas gulf coast. This enterprise netted all three men a sizable fortune. With his profits, Don Francisco established the first bank in south Texas at Brownsville and Matamoras. At the conclusion of the war, the activities of all three men were found by the United States to have been unpatriotic, consequently to avoid retribution from the Yankee Government, all three men moved across the border and lived in self imposed exile in Matamoras, Mexico for two years. All three were granted full pardons by U. S. President Andrew Jackson and they returned to Texas and resumed their business ventures.

Don Francisco Yturria was the recipient of a large land grant of more than 340 Leagues, (150,000 acres) of land in south Texas. This ranch land is presently located in Cameron, Willacy, Kenedy and Starr counties. Don Francisco died in 1912. Today, his great grandsons, Frank and Fausto Yturria and his great grand daughter, Stella Garcia .Zarate all live either on a portion of the remaining acreage of the massive ranch or in Brownsville where Fausto and Frank have multiple business interests. All of Don Francisco's heirs have used their inheritances wisely and have made huge contributions to the history of Texas and their fellow Texans.

CHAPTER 34

TEXANS AND POLITICS

. Texas entered the 20th century still a relative youngster in- so-far as politics was concerned. Their political experiences were to be if not informative, at least they were interesting. One engaging thing about most Texans is their sense of humor. Politics has always seemed to bring forth that humor. They are prone to be very forgiving if, in their opinion, the politician is usually well intentioned. They will forgive mistakes in judgment so long as they are convinced that the person is moral in his/her intentions

In 1914, one of the most colorful Governors in Texas history, James E. (Farmer Jim) Ferguson was elected. In 1915, border problems in the Lower Rio Grande Valley came to a head. A Mexican national was arrested in Brownsville carrying a document calling for "Mexicans, Indians, Japanese and Blacks" to rise up and massacre all Anglo males. The discovery of the manifesto caused a blood bath in South Texas. Many innocent Mexican Nationals and Mexican-Americans were killed. Mexican soldiers from Matamoros participated in raids on Anglos north of the border. Governor Ferguson sent in the Texas Rangers to quell the trouble. Governor Ferguson met with the Mexican President, Venustiano Carranza in Laredo in an effort to settle the matter and attempt to improve relations. The raids continued.

President Woodrow Wilson determined that the hostilities were serious and activated the Texas National Guard. Pancho Villa attacked Columbus, New Mexico and two villages in Texas, Glenn Springs and Boquillas on the Rio Grande. General John J. Pershing, aided by Lieutenant Douglas Mc Arthur under his command, pursued Pancho Villa deep into Mexico but failed to capture him. The raids by Mexican Banditos continued, but were much diminished. Texas was not entirely at peace but hostilities with Mexico abated considerably.

In 1917 Ferguson was impeached for misappropriation and misapplication of state funds in the infamous "Chicken Salad Case." He was found guilty and impeached by the Texas Senate for using state treasury funds for the purchase of foodstuffs and other personal items. He resigned as Governor the day before his impeachment was to be effective and proclaimed that the impeachment "did not apply to him." The legislature barred him from ever again serving in any public office in Texas. Apparently, a lot of Texans were not greatly offended by his exploits. To circumvent the law enacted by the legislature, he twice ran his wife, Miriam, also known as "Ma" Ferguson, in two successful political campaigns for Governor of Texas, in1925 and again in 1933. It was generally accepted that "Ma" Ferguson was no more than a "stand-in" for her husband. Although "Farmer Jim" gained considerable fame and acceptance among the farmers in Texas, he was no great hero to most Texans.

Texas has elected a variety of "interesting" people to state-wide office. W. Lee O'Daniel, nicknamed, "Pass the biscuits Pappy," although not a native son of Texas, leap-frogged his way to the Governor's mansion as a flour salesman for Burris Mills on an Austin radio station. Pappy was elected Governor in 1939. O'Daniel, accompanied by Bob Wills and his band, The Light Crust Doughboys, was a major fixture on Texas radio, delighting the primarily rural audiences with biblical quotations and home spun songs and humor. Bob Wills soon tired of his $15.00 per week job with "Pappy" O'Daniel, as did his band, and they quit.

Bob took his band on the road under the name of "Bob Wills and the former Light Crust Doughboys". O'Daniel hired a bevy of high priced lawyers to sue Bob Wills for illegally using the "Light Crust Doughboys" name. Eventually the law suit was settled through arbitration. Bob Wills dropped the Light Crust Doughboys moniker for his band and they became known as "Bob Wills, King of Swing." No one, even to this day, has ever questioned Bob Wills' status as "King of Swing" in Texas.

Although he was a totally ineffective Governor, it proved to be no obstacle to W. Lee O' Daniel's aspirations to higher office. The desire by business-men to get rid of "Pappy" as Governor, was so strong that they banded together, pooling their resources and backed his candidacy against Congressman Lyndon Johnson, among others, for the U. S. Senate. He was elected in 1941 and served two terms as a U. S. Senator from Texas where, to no one's surprise, he was equally as ineffective as he had been as Governor. He had been far more effective as a flour salesman than he was as a politician.

CHAPTER 35

A FEW CLAIMS TO FAME (OR INFAMY)

There have been any number of Texans that gained their fame through their exploits on the wrong side of the law. In the 1930's, Clyde Barrow and Bonnie Parker, made even more infamous by the movie "Bonnie and Clyde", cut a swath of lawlessness and murder across Texas, Oklahoma, Kansas, Indiana, Ohio, Arkansas and Louisiana. The movie portrayed them as modern day "Robin Hoods" rather than modern day "Jack the Rippers," which would have been far more accurate in view of their heinous deeds. In 1934, a Texas Ranger, Captain Frank Hamer was given the task of bringing Bonnie and Clyde to justice. Hamer, acutely aware of the reputation of the two outlaws and their vow not to be taken alive, decided to set up an ambush for them. Tipped off that Bonnie and Clyde were in the area of western Louisiana, near Shreveport, he enlisted the assistance of the Louisiana Law Enforcement. They meted out quick justice at Gibsland, Louisiana in the ambush. Captain Hamer brought their bodies back to Dallas and put them on public display to show other aspiring desperados that there was little chance of escaping a Texas Ranger's long reach.

A few of our outstanding personalities were found to be a bit on the shady side of the law. Two characters stand out in Texas history as either the most famous or infamous local politicians in the state of Texas. Archie Parr, and after his death, his son George Parr was the unofficial "Duke of Duval County", with the County Seat at San Diego. Archie Parr moved to Duval County in the early 1900's. He quickly learned to speak Spanish and with the large Spanish-speaking Mexican population in Duval County, he was soon elected County Judge. Archie Parr and later his son and political heir George Parr, ran Duval County for years with an iron fist as a virtual fiefdom. County money and Parr money were virtually indistinguishable. Every serious Democratic candidate for statewide or national office sought out the "Duke," and tried to gain his support. During elections the Parrs, or their henchmen, would take fists full of money around to the Mexican population of Duval County to pay their Texas $2.00 Poll Tax and a dollar or two for their trouble and just to make sure that they made it to the polls and voted. If an insufficient number of voters turned out to assure the election of Parr's favorite, it was a simple matter to pluck names from the local cemetery to make up the deficiency. George Parr was later convicted of fraud and sentenced to several years in prison. A few days before he was to surrender to the authorities to begin serving his sentence, he committed suicide at his ranch.

Billie Sol Estes is a name that in Texas is almost synonymous with fraud and corruption. A free wheeler and scam artist, within a few short years, Billie Sol became one of the wealthiest men in West Texas. He parlayed ownership of a few anhydrous ammonia tanks, used by farmers to fertilize their crops through irrigation, into a huge fortune by securing loans from several banks on hundreds of nonexistent tanks. Billie Sol would take a banker out to his farm, show him several hundred tanks, and then to a long lunch with libations. After lunch they would visit yet another farm to inspect more tanks. While they had been at lunch, Billie Sol's men would have cut the serial numbers from the batch of tanks at the first farm, attached new serial numbers and moved the tanks to the second farm. He further feathered his nest to the tune of over twenty-one million bucks a year through bogus cotton allotments and farm subsidies, and for growing and storing non-existent cotton bales. When rumors began circulating that Billie Sol's agricultural subsidies were not exactly on the "up and up", Henry Marshall, a federal Department of Agriculture official, who had approved Billie Sol's cotton allotments, began an investigation and was soon found dead. The official cause of death was ruled suicide.

His death was the result of a case of severe lead poisoning from five bullets to the head fired from a bolt action 22 caliber, bolt action rifle. From the evidence it would appear that Mr. Marshall was an accomplished contortionist with agile toes, else he could not have fired and reloaded a bolt action rifle, then fired and reloaded four more times into his own head within nanoseconds as he lay dying.

Rumor has it that Billie Sol Estes' connections reached all the way to Washington D. C. and into the office of then Vice President Lyndon B. Johnson. He was convicted of a federal crime of fraud and sentenced to fifteen years in prison. When released from prison he "got religion" and, through his attorney, volunteered to "come clean" and tell a tale of corruption, murder, and intrigue, implicating several officials in high office, in exchange for immunity and a pardon. All of the people that Mr. Estes has claimed were implicated have now gone to meet their maker. The wheels of justice grind exceedingly slow in Texas as well as in other parts of the world, which occasionally works to the benefit of the other suspected principal actors.

Another infamous Texas oil tycoon, Clinton Manges, was not even a Texan. He was born in Oklahoma but preferred to be known as a Texan. He was at one time considered to be the richest man in Texas. He supposedly owned more than 100,000 acres of ranch land in Duval County. He also claimed to have owned leases of mineral rights on more than 400,000 acres of proven oil reserves. He grew up a poor boy. As a young man he is said to have picked cotton for a living. Later, he worked for a cotton gin at Raymondville, Texas. He began accumulating his wealth by leveraging his credit to the maximum. He owned the now defunct Gunslingers football franchise in the United States Football League. He lost the franchise in 1985 when he failed to meet his club's payrolls. He was intimate friends with many of the leading politicians of the State. He weathered several legal battles, including a dispute with Mobil Oil Company over oil and gas leases on the 72,000 Guerra Ranch in Duval County. He died in September, 2010 from various forms of cancer. His daughter once remarked that "Anyone else would have died years earlier, but my father was an example of how far being an ornery old "bastard" can take you."

T. Cullen Davis was an heir to a huge "Oil Patch" fortune. His family owned Midcontinent Oil Field Supply Company, and other interests in the oil field and oil field supply business. He will be best remembered for having been arrested and charged with the murders of his stepdaughter and his estranged wife's boyfriend. He hired the most noted and flamboyant criminal defense attorney in the state, Racehorse Haynes, as his defense attorney, commenting that he wanted "The Best Justice money can buy". Cullen Davis' wife, Priscilla, filed for divorce. The divorce proceedings dragged on for years. After "one of the most expensive murder investigations and trials in Texas history", the jury found Davis not guilty. Davis was again arrested a couple of years later for hiring a hit man to murder both his wife Priscilla and the Judge of the ongoing divorce trial. Racehorse Haynes again pulled a rabbit out of his bag of tricks and Davis was again acquitted. Cullen Davis does not come close to qualifying as an honorable Texan, but his exploits have earned him dishonorable mention, and his attorney considerable fame.

CHAPTER 36

A FEW TEXAS "OLD COOTS"

. "Coot": defined by the Random House College Dictionary as: 1.Formal: "Any aquatic bird of the genus of Faluca as f. Americana of North America and f. atra of the Old World, characterized by oblate toes, short wings and tail. 3. Informal: "A foolish and crotchety old man".

The fact that Texans are a different breed of the human species and that they are unique, naturally produces a variety of eccentric, or down-right crotchety people. (It is not necessary for the human "Coot" to have long, funny toes or short wings and a tail). This sets Texans apart from most other Americans born and reared in other states. The determination of who is or is not an "Old Coot" is not a designation bestowed by some committee, group of journalists, or commentators. It is an individual determination. Like beauty, the status of being an "Old Coot" or not, is in the eye of the beholder. A goodly number of old time Texans are, or were, as the case may be, in the Texas vernacular, "Old Coots." Old Coot status cannot be conferred on one until the minimum age of fifty or so. Once you know what to look for you can spot an old "coot" at a hundred and fifty yards in a crowd. He can be either tall or short. He might be wearing an old beat up five X Stetson hat, (in the old days, the price of Stetson Hats was $20.00 per "X"), sweat-stained and most often dusty, the brim rolled to a certain angle and pulled down to just above the eyes which will be squinty and kind of "scrunched up". Likely as not, he'll be holding his listeners spell bound with one of his yarns. An unspoken rule to qualify as an "Old Coot," is that one must be crotchety and must have a fair amount of contrariness about him and be circumspect in discussing one's business propositions. He'll start out a business deal with "Now I don't reckon you'd be interested in", what ever it is he is interested in swapping, buying, selling or trading. He can say no without ever saying "no" and you know he has said "no" without having hurt your feelings. Unless he is teed off, he will have a twinkle in his eyes. If he is teed off, his eyes will be like two pin pricks of hard steel and you had best steer clear for a while.

An Old Coot always doffs his hat to ladies, if he is wearing one. In public, all females are ladies to him even though she might be a known "Lady of The Night". He never calls a stranger, man or woman, by their first name until he has known them for a good long spell and has decided that they are worthy of his acknowledgment. It will be Mister so-and-so or Mrs. or Miss so-and-so. Being called by your first name by an Old Coot is the equivalent of him calling you his friend. When addressing an Old Coot, if you are under twenty years of age, and he hasn't given you permission to call him by his first name, you had best call him "Mister" or those merry eyes will turn to two pin pricks of hard steel and you will feel as though a Texas "blue norther" has just passed through causing an extreme drop in the ambient temperature.

He will have no butt and the seat of his pants will look as though a litter of piglets and a sow have moved out. Every button but the collar will be buttoned unless he is wearing a bolo, or in rare cases, "an eastern tie," worn only by Bankers and Lawyers. If you are around him for any length of time, unless it's a Sunday, you may be invited to have a "Jack and branch water" with him. Should you encounter him on a Sunday, he will have swapped his twenty-five year old-sweat stained Stetson for a pristine, freshly cleaned and blocked ten X Stetson with the brim rolled to just the right angle and a "kick" in the front crown. His western cut shirt will be starched and freshly ironed, his jeans will have a crease down the exact middle of his pants leg and his boots will shine like mirrors. He will have on a modest, western belt with a few silver ornaments around it, and no fancy huge rodeo buckle; those are for wannabes. If he is a "lawyer type", he will probably have on a suit and boots, but most likely a bolo instead of a "tie." One thing that won't be changed is his demeanor. On Sunday, most likely he will have a twinkle in his eyes. Old Coots rarely exercise their right to hold grudges on Sundays. And Old Coots never, ever, wear their hat beyond the front door of a home or restaurant. If there is a "wannabe" cowboy with his hat or cap on in a home or restaurant, he has not been properly reared or taught good manners, regardless of his age. Old Coots are a pleasure to do business with, even when they get the best of you. Many of the old time ranchers, farmers, a few business men and lawyer types, but only a very small number of politicians, can be legitimately referred to as "Old Coots,". (If you care to research what constitutes an "Old Coot" you can refer to the May 1987 issue of the Texas "National" Magazine, The Texas Monthly, for a description of this human phenomenon. Last, but not least, an "Old Coot" must have developed the reputation among his peers of being "half-way honest". There are even some lawyers that managed to earn this reputation.

We have had a good many old coots during the 20th century. The thirty-fourth President of the United States, Dwight David Eisenhower was born in Denison, Texas where his birth place is now a National Landmark. It is questionable how much influence being born in Texas had on his life and career, in view of the fact that the Eisenhower family moved from Texas to Abilene, Kansas when Dwight David was only two years old. Not surprisingly, General Eisenhower enthusiastically invoked his birth right as a Texan during his 1952 campaign for the Presidency. One thing about being born a Texan is that no one has to ask you if you are a Texan. If you are you'll tell them within the first two minutes and if you are not you don't want to be embarrassed by saying so. "Ike" qualifies for the status of being a "Native Texan". He just could never dress properly and never learned to speak the language to attain the status in Texas as an "Old Coot".. It is beyond one's comprehension to imagine Ike wearing a Stetson hat, cowboy boots, and saying that "I'll gar-ron-damn-tee ya that I am fixin to" do something. In addition, he had too much "butt" to be a legitimate "Old Texas Coot."

There have been several "self proclaimed Texans" that used their adopted heritage to their benefit. Sam Rayburn, from Bonham, Texas, was born in Tennessee and moved to Texas at the tender age of five. Elected as a U.S. Congressman, "Mr. Sam", as he was most affectionately referred to, served as Speaker of the U. S. House of Representatives for almost seventeen years, longer than any other Speaker in American history. He also served as a member of the House for forty-nine consecutive years; longer than any house member in history. Sam Rayburn and his counterpart in the U. S. Senate, Senate, Majority Leader Lyndon B. Johnson, were said to have been the most politically powerful duo in our history. During a vote in the House of Representatives, Mr. Sam was noted for banging his gavel at the appropriate time and shouting into the microphone "the ayes (or nays as the case might be) have it," with little or no attention being given to the vote. Only a roll call vote could over-turn Mr. Sam's gavel but very few House Members ever had the guts to call for one. Mr. Sam walked the walk, talked the talk and sometimes dressed the part, but not being a native son, could not legitimately be referred to as an "Old Coot"..

John Nance (Cactus Jack) Garner from Uvalde was President Franklin D. Roosevelt's Vice President. Garner is remembered chiefly for his observation that the office of Vice President was about as worthless as "a warm bucket of spit." Most Texans agree that his verbatim statement referred to the use of another part of one's anatomy rather than the mouth. Former Vice President Cactus Jack Garner was as irascible and as crotchety as one would expect from an old coot. Vice President Garner was a well qualified, genuine, "Old Coot"

Lyndon Baines Johnson was born August 27, 1908 near Stonewall, Texas, he was elected to the U.S. House of Representatives in 1937. He ran unsuccessfully for the US Senate in 1941 and was defeated by W. Lee "Pass The Biscuits Pappy" O'Daniel, former Governor of Texas.

In 1948, Johnson once again ran for the U.S. Senate against a field of ten candidates in the Democratic primary. In the run off election between Lyndon Johnson and former Governor Coke Stevenson, the votes showed Lyndon Johnson ahead by some 40 odd votes. Governor Stevenson called for a recount of all ballots. It was found that the ballot count of the famous/infamous box thirteen from Duval County was questionable. If all ballots were legitimate, it assured Johnson the smallest majority vote between two candidates in Texas history. A mere switch of some twenty or thirty votes would have given Stevenson a victory. Governor Stevenson and an assistant, former

Texas Ranger Frank Hamer, went to the bank in Alice, Texas, county seat of Jim Wells County, where the ballot boxes had been impounded. Deputy Sheriffs required both men to surrender all of their writing material, pencils, paper, or anything that could be used to record what was contained in the ballot box. All of this was done under the watchful eye of the "Duke of Duval County," Archie Parr. There were 204 ballots in "Box 13," and 203 of them were for Lyndon Johnson and one for Coke Stevenson. All of Lyndon Johnson's votes were in perfect alphabetical order. A majority of the names on the ballots also appeared on an equal number of tombstones in the San Diego cemetery, the county seat of Duval County, Archie Parr's home county. Lyndon Johnson's friends point out that in the Mexican culture, some families are quite large and often several families will have the same family name although not related. Many Texans still claim that enough deceased people from Duval County were miraculously resurrected to vote and settle the election.

The final decision rested with a Federal Judge from Fort. Worth appointed by Lyndon's good friend and mentor, President Franklin D. Roosevelt. The Federal Court ruled that Lyndon B. Johnson was the winner of the election by the slimmest majority of eighty-seven votes. Many Texans still argue that the election was won "Parr style".

Johnson was elected Senate Majority Leader in 1955. Paired with "Mr. Sam" Rayburn, Speaker of the House, they soon became the most formidable members of either of the two Houses of Congress.

Lyndon Johnson was a democratic candidate for President in the primary of 1960 but lost his bid for the nomination to Senator John F. Kennedy. Figuring that he needed a Texan on the ballot in order to win, Kennedy invited "LBJ" to run on his ticket as Vice President. The choice insured the Texas vote would "go all the way with

JFK". Before the end of JFK's first term, Vice President Lyndon Johnson was to become our thirty-sixth President. He was sworn into office aboard Air Force One, in Dallas, Texas by Federal Judge Sarah Hughes immediately following the assassination of President John F. Kennedy in Dallas, Texas on November 22, 1963. Vice President Johnson happened to have a copy of the President's oath of office, which he produced from his coat pocket when Judge Hughes was unable to recall the words of the oath. (It was rumored that he kept the oath handy "just in case").

Among his eccentricities, President Johnson developed a penchant for swimming in the White House swimming pool naked as a jay bird while conversing with his high ranking military officers and other officials about the Vietnam war. No doubt about it, President Lyndon Johnson was a genuine Texas "Old Coot"

One of the most unlikely politicians to pounce upon the Texas stage was a billionaire named H. Ross Perot. Ross was born in Texarkana, Texas. He was a graduate of the United States Naval Academy and was instrumental in establishing the Academy's honor system. He served his four year commitment and then resigned his commission out of discontent with the Navy. He worked for IBM until 1962, became disillusioned with the company and quit to start his own business, Electronic Data Systems. Ross solicited government contracts and was turned down seventy-seven times before he got his first government contract. He eventually acquired the extremely lucrative contract to computerize Medicare records. He took his company, EDS, public in 1968 and the Wall Street stock price sky rocketed from $16 per share to $160 per share in a matter of days. In 1984 he sold controlling interest in EDS to General Motors for $2.4 billion dollars. In 1988, Fortune Magazine labeled Ross Perot the "fastest, richest

Texan." Ross Perot will be well remembered for rescuing two EDS employees from Iran following the Iranian Revolution. It was a risky exercise, but typical of Texans ingenuity. In 1992, Ross Perot announced that he was a candidate for President of the United States as an Independent. He later threatened to withdraw his candidacy, claiming that opponents had threatened to reveal compromising photographs of his daughter. It was soon revealed that the threat was a hoax and he continued his campaign for the Presidency. In his efforts, he spent an estimated $12.3 million of his own money. He lost the campaign to George H. W. Bush in the Republican Primary by a margin of 18.9% of Republican votes for Perot to 43.39% of Republican votes for Bush. He registered and ran in the General Election as an Independent candidate, labeled by critics as a "spoiler candidate." An analysis of exit polls indicated that Perot drew 38% of his vote from George H. W. Bush and 38% of his vote from Bill Clinton. Clinton won the election by a majority of the popular vote 43.0 % to Bush's 37.4%. Perot's critics claimed that without Perot in the race, Bush would have won by a large majority. Perot denied the charges, but since then has distanced himself from most political activities.

Although he usually doesn't dress the part, Ross Perot can rightfully claim the distinction of being a true unique crotchety and contrary Texas Old Coot.

It has already been noted that when Texas really needed strong, level-headed leadership, such a person has seemed to always come forward. During the 1970's, a very serious bank fraud case, dubbed "The Sharpestown Scandal" erupted involving Texas Governor Preston Smith and several other high ranking officials in the Smith administration. The reputation of the State Government of Texas was at an all time low. A successful Rancher, Dolph Briscoe, Jr., from Uvalde, the home town of former Vice President John Nance Garner, decided to run as a reform candidate for Governor against several other Democrats, the most notable two; sitting Governor Preston Smith and Lieutenant Governor Ben Barnes. Dolph Briscoe ran on a platform of honesty and integrity in state government and opposition to any new state taxes. He was handily elected. His first term was for two years. During his first term the state legislature passed a constitutional amendment changing the term to four years. In his first term he focused on increasing the efficiency of the existing state government and strongly opposed the creation of new state agencies.

Briscoe, a very successful rancher, was a member of the Texas and Southwestern Cattlemen's Association. During his administration, with the help of the Association, and Briscoe's aid in securing state and federal assistance, the United States Department of Agriculture began the highly successful program for the eradication of the screw worm, a plague upon farmers and cattlemen. This program saved farmers and ranchers on both sides of the Rio Grande hundreds of millions of dollars. The program is being continued to the present time to assure that there is no resurgence of the problem. Dolph Briscoe was a well respected governor. During his administration, thousands of miles of farm-to-market and ranch-to-market roads were built in Texas to enable farmers and ranchers to move their cattle, produce and cotton to market in all kinds of weather. The only blemish on his record occurred in 1978 during his second term. Briscoe, using his political power, had named practically every appointed person in state government. He relied on his appointments secretary to secure for his consideration, the names of the most outstanding Texans to serve in those positions. Briscoe wasn't aware of it, but his secretary had made a terrible mistake. As a result Governor Briscoe appointed a very well-qualified, but a dead man to the State Health Advisory Commission. His critics had a grand time over this embarrassing mistake. The Texas Monthly Magazine awarded him the "Bum

Steer Award" for the comical aspects of the appointment. Dolph Briscoe, Jr. was the last Texas Governor to serve under the two year term and the first to serve under the four year term. During his administration there were no new taxes. When he passed away in 2010, he was the single largest land holder in Texas, owning ranches through-out the state. An honest and honorable man, Dolph Briscoe, Jr. was a true Texan and a verifiable Old Coot.

CHAPTER 37

TEXAS LADIES AND AMERICAN ICONS

Sandra Day O'Conner was born in El Paso, Texas in 1930. She spent summers on her parent's ranch in Arizona. She attended a private school in El Paso and graduated from El Paso's Austin High School. She graduated at the tender age of sixteen. The Arizona ranch had no electricity or running water. Sandra Day grew up in the rough and tumble life of the ranch. She assisted in branding cattle and repairing what-ever needed repair on the ranch among other duties. She quickly learned that whatever was broken had to be fixed and often there was no one handy but her to fix it. After graduating from Law School, she soon learned first hand about prejudices against women, especially in the legal profession. In 1969, Arizona Governor Williams appointed Sandra to fill the unexpired term of a State Senator who had resigned. In 1970 she was elected in her own right to the seat and reelected in 1972. She was the first woman to serve as the

Majority Leader in the State Senate. In 1981 President Ronald Reagan appointed Sandra Day O'Connor to the United States Supreme Court. She was quickly and unanimously confirmed as the first female Justice in American history. She served on the United States Supreme Court with honor and distinction. She retired from the highest Court in the land in 2006. A truly great lady, an Icon and an example for all Americans. She has proven that when you set your mind to it and work hard enough, you can over-come any obstacle and accomplish whatever your heart desires. A truly great native Texas lady.

United States Ambassador to the United Kingdom! That is an impressive title. Anne Legendre Armstrong is the first and only lady to have served her country as our Ambassador to our greatest friend and ally, the United Kingdom of Great Britain. She was appointed Ambassador to "The Court of St. James," or as is more commonly known, Great Britain, in 1976. Anne was born

Anne Legendre in New Orleans, Louisiana. She was a graduate of Vassar, class of 1949. In 1950 she married Tobin Armstrong, grandson of John B. Armstrong, and an heir to one of the oldest ranching families in Texas. Anne, a life- long Republican, started in politics as a precinct worker. She moved up through the political ranks to become vice chairman of the state Republican Party and later, chairwoman of the Republican National Committee. She was the keynote speaker at the 1972 Republican convention, the first woman of either party, up until that time, to deliver a political party's keynote address. She served on the boards of several well known American Corporations. She was the recipient of the Presidential Medal of Freedom awarded to her by President Ronald Reagan. Her husband, Tobin Armstrong, did himself, the state of Texas and the American people, a huge favor when he met and married Anne Legendre Armstrong. Sadly, she passed away suffering from cancer at 80 years of age on July 30, 2008. Truly, one of the great ladies of

America. Tobin Armstrong, Anne's husband was a very successful rancher and horse breeder and was famous in his own right. In addition to breeding and raising cattle, his ranch bred and trained polo ponies. His Grandfather, John B. Armstrong, was the famous Texas Ranger who captured John Wesley Hardin, the infamous outlaw. His brother was John B. Armstrong, Jr., President and General Manager of the huge King Ranch for many years until his death. Tobin was a skilled polo player. His polo ponies were in great demand all over the world, wherever polo was played. Tobin passed away October 7, 2005.

There have been many ladies in Texas history that deserve honorable mention. Ann Richards, was a real political firebrand. Ann won a hard fought, no holds barred fight, with Clayton Williams to become Governor of Texas in 1991. She will be best remembered for her quote of a previous Governor about English being the officially recognized primary language in Texas: "If English was good enough for Jesus Christ, it ought to be good enough for the children of Texas." Clayton Williams will be remembered for his quip: "If you are gonna be raped anyway, you just as well lie back and enjoy it." This bawdy and vulgar remark had considerable bearing on his loss of the election.

CHAPTER 38

A FEW NATIVE SONS

A great many of our notable personalities have become famous in their chosen fields of endeavor. One proud, native son of Texas that only semi-qualifies for the title of an Old Coot. is the noted Author and Historian, T. R. Fehrenbach. Mr. Fehrenbach lacks the qualification of being foolish, to fit the full definition of an Old Coot, but he does have the required "crotchetiness" to at least earn a place among other famous and not so famous Old Coots. Born in San Benito Texas, a Korean War Veteran, he has authored at least eighteen non-fiction books, many of which were and still are, best sellers. His History of Mexico, "Fire and Blood," and his highly acclaimed History of Texas, "Lone Star," are books that should be required reading for all students at the High School level and on into their college years. That is if they really want to know the true history of Texas.

Clint Murchison had most of the requirements and could have eventually been rewarded the honor of "Old Coot". He forfeited any opportunity for the honor when he up and sold our very own "America's Team", The Dallas Cowboys, to a super egoist non-Texan, who, before the ink was dry on the contract of sale, fired the best damn football coach known to man or woman, Tom Landry, a native son of Mission Texas. Tom Landry did deserve the well-earned honor of being an "Old Coot." The only other Pro Football Coach to deserve this honor was "Bum" Phillips, former head coach of the former Houston Oilers. Who knows? Had Bum Phillips been allowed to continue to lead and direct the Oilers, they might still be Oilers and still be in Houston.

H. L. Hunt was not a native-born Texan, so in spite of all of his accomplishments and shenanigans, such as being married to two women at the same time without the benefit of divorce and getting away with it, his one-time title of the "Richest Man in the World", his well known contrariness and idiosyncrasies, he could never attain the status as a legitimate Old Coot.

H. L. Hunt's youngest son, Lamar Hunt gained a modicum of fame in Texas by organizing and financing the Dallas Texans pro football team and was the prime mover in creating the American Football League. The Dallas Texans will be best remembered for the 1962 Championship game against the Houston Oilers. It was the first game in history to go into not only double overtime, but into the fifth overtime. Two minutes and seventeen seconds into the fifth overtime, Tommy Brooker scored a twenty-five yard field goal to end the game with a score of twenty to seventeen over the Oilers. Frustrated that the Dallas Texans were failing to attract the Dallas fans' support equal to the Dallas Cowboys, Lamar moved the ball club to Kansas City and renamed them the Kansas City Chiefs. Mr. Hunt's other two boys can best be remembered for their efforts to corner the silver market, for which the long arm of the law stepped in and meted out justice in their case.

Richard, "Racehorse" Haynes, more rightfully belongs on the famous side of the ledger. He was born a poor boy in San Antonio. He earned the nickname of "Racehorse" on the football field while in Junior High. He spent his summers working in the oil fields, and won a scholarship to the University of Houston. He served two stints in the military, one in the Navy, where he was decorated for heroics at Iwo Jima and then as an Army Paratrooper. He earned his law degree from Bates College of Law in 1956. Racehorse was a protégé of a legal legend, Percy Foremen. He never shied away from taking big, complicated cases. He successfully defended Dr. John Hill, a Houston plastic surgeon, accused of murdering his wealthy socialite wife. When asked if he was the best criminal defense lawyer in Texas, he answered: "I believe I am, but why do you restrict me to Texas"? He had already successfully defended Cullen

Davis in two separate and different murder charges and won both times. Racehorse Haynes is a unique Texan, lawyer and human being. He deserves the title of "the most irascible lawyer in Texas."

Joe Jamail is known as America's King of Torts. If you are the head of a corporation, no matter how rich your balance sheet is, or how extensive your stable of corporate lawyers, if your company receives notice of a pending law suit and the name of Joe Jamail pops up as the plaintiff's attorney, it can immediately turn your blood to ice water and ruin your day. Your worst nightmare has been realized. Joe Jamail did not earn the moniker of "King of Torts" accidentally. Just ask Texaco Corporation. Joe turned an unwritten gentlemen's agreement and hand shake into a $11 billion dollar nightmare for Texaco and the largest monetary jury award victory for Pennzoil and their lawyer in history. Although the suit was eventually settled for $3 billion, Joe Jamail's contingency fee was large enough to earn him the reputation of Texas' richest lawyer. Remington Arms and the manufacturer of the Japanese automobile import, Honda, can both attest to Joe's effectiveness before a jury. Joe Jamail is uniquely qualified for the honor of being referred to as A Rich Old Coot

Major General Claire Chennault, born at Commerce, Texas, gained fame as the leader of the quasi American Expeditionary Force of pilots in China known as the "Flying Tigers" during World War II. There is no doubt that China was saved from total defeat by Japan prior to and during World War II by Chennault's Flying Tigers. Born September, 1896 at Commerce, Texas, Chennault was related to both Texas' General Sam Houston and Virginias' Robert E. Lee.

Fleet Admiral Chester W. Nimitz, the man who was the architect of our successful war in the Pacific theater during World War II, was born in Fredericksburg, Texas. His family owned and operated a hotel in Fredericksburg that was constructed to resemble the prow of a ship. It is the home of the outstanding museum honoring Nimitz and the battles for the Pacific. It is well worth the cost, time and effort to visit. Admiral Nimitz was one of the signers for the Allied Forces of the document of unconditional surrender of the Japanese in Tokyo Bay on September 2, 1945 aboard the Battleship "Missouri." Well loved and respected by thousands of sailors and Marines for his direction of the Pacific War, Admiral Nimitz may not have dressed the part, but there is no doubt that he was a real Texan and an "Old Coot".

CHAPTER 39

SOME NOTABLE ENTREPANEURS

"RED MCCOMBS"

One of the world's richest men, "Red" McCombs, was born in the small village of Spur, Texas, located a few miles east of Lubbock on the Texas plains. The nickname "Red" comes about because of his flaming red hair. Red was a talented athlete and did a short stint as a lineman on the football team at Southwestern University at Georgetown, Texas. He served in the U. S. Army for two years, 1946 and 1947. When he returned to civilian life he entered the University of Texas at Austin where he majored in business and then went to law school. In the early 1950's he left college to sell automobiles in Corpus Christi where he met and teamed up with another car salesman, Austin Hemphill. Together they moved to San Antonio and formed the Hemphill-McCombs Ford Agency which was to become the foundation for Red's huge Automotive Group.

Red McCombs has since been involved in the energy business in Houston, the real estate development business, ownership of radio station WOAI in San Antonio and Clear Channel Communications. With a partner he purchased the struggling basket ball team, The Dallas Chaparrals. They moved the team to San Antonio where they renamed the team "The San Antonio Spurs". The team became an instant hit in the NBA. He has owned the Minnesota Vikings football team, and, among other ventures, has been involved in thoroughbred racing as a major partner in Walmac Farms of Lexington, Kentucky.

In each of his many endeavors Red McCombs has succeeded beyond his wildest hopes. He has been a major contributor to his Alma Mater, the University of Texas, donating fifty million dollars to the school of business. Red ranked as the 913th richest man in the world by Forbes Magazine. His entrepreneurial spirit and business accomplishments along with his philanthropy, has had a huge influence on Texas. He is the epitome of a real Texan

T. BOONE PICKENS

T. Boone Pickens was not born a Texan. He is, however, a true, bona fide, Texas entrepreneur extraordinaire. Mr. Pickens was born and reared in Oklahoma and graduated from Oklahoma State University at Stillwater. When the Oklahoma oil boom ended in the 1930's, Boone's father had the good sense to move his family to Amarillo, Texas. Boone did attend Texas A&M on a basketball scholarship. He lost his scholarship and transferred to Oklahoma State University. He graduated with a degree in geology. In 1956, after a short stint as an oilfield wildcatter, he founded a company which later became his flagship company; Mesa Petroleum. By 1981 Mesa had become one of the largest independent oil companies in the world. Boone shifted his interest to acquiring other oil and gas companies. His corporate acquisitions soon earned him the reputation as a "corporate raider". In a few years he had a net worth of over $1 billion dollars. A fortune that would be considered worth five times that much on today's monetary market.

As his fortune grew, his philanthropic gifts to charities and to universities grew. Along with several other billionaires, he pledged to give away to charitable institutions and institutions of higher learning, at least half of his net worth. True to his pledge, he donated millions of dollars to Oklahoma State University. In May 2007, he donated $5 million to the University of Texas at Dallas to fund education and research in the area of brain science. In August, 2007 he donated $5 million to the Downtown Dallas YMCA. T. Boone Pickens has returned much of his wealth to his alma mater and the state of his birth and a good deal of his money to his adopted state of Texas. T, Boone Pickens, while not a native born Texan, has done both himself and Texas proud.

HERB KELLEHER

Herb Kelleher, founder and former CEO of Southwest Airlines, migrated to Texas and landed in Austin to set up shop in the lawyering business. While having dinner with businessman Rollin King, the two of them sketched out on a cocktail napkin, the outline of a concept that would become Southwest Airlines. It took the two budding entrepreneurs over a year to overcome the legal challenges from competitors intent on seeing that Southwest Airlines never got off the ground. Once airborne, Southwest Airlines succeeded beyond anyone's expectations. They succeeded by daring to be different. They began by offering their passengers lower fares. They eliminated unnecessary frills, avoided the overcrowded hub airports, and developed a scheduling system different from other airlines. By using secondary airports, Southwest cut the turn-around time for their airplanes at airports to less than half of their competitors. Their innovations allowed Southwest to better utilize their aircraft more profitably than other airlines. Just as many interstate trucking companies had learned, Herb Kelleher began the system of "being lopaded in both directions". Southwest's low fares filled the seating capacity of almost every flight, proving that full utilization of their equipment would allow them to lower their fares and still make a profit. Southwest's advertising slogan was "We Fly For Peanuts" and served only beverages and specially packaged bags of Southwest Airlines peanuts. Their crews are friendly, efficient, interested in their job and "their company" and take their jobs seriously. When time allows Herb Kelleher to do so, it is not a bit unusual to find him on just about any of their flights, sitting down with passengers, sharing their peanuts and joking with the crew.

Herb Kelleher and Southwest Airlines has revolutionized airline travel, and has been responsible for much lower rates and better scheduling by competing airlines. And, he started it all right here in Texas! A very astute corporate CEO! Herb Kelleher wasn't born a Texan, but otherwise he has all of the qualifications so typical of native Texans.

CHAPTER 40

JUST A FEW TEXAS ARTISTS

Texas has produced its fair share of world famous artists. The greatest classical pianist of all time, while not born a Texan, was adopted by Texans soon after his arrival. Texans have no qualms about adopting "a foreign born" and claiming him or her as their very own. Kilgore, Texas was originally semi-famous for its proliferation of oil derricks. In downtown Kilgore, for many years oil derricks were almost as thick as the hair on a dog's back. Along about 1940, an event took place that in the future was to bring world- wide attention to the small town. The Cliburn family moved from Shreveport, Louisiana to Kilgore with a six year old son named Van. Few residents of the small town, outside his family, realized that there was a world famous pianist in the making among them. In 1958, after winning many piano competitions throughout Texas and attending the prestigious Julliard

School in New York, Van Cliburn was invited to Moscow, Russia, to participate in, and where he won the famous world-wide Tchaikovsky Piano Competition. Kilgore immediately claimed him as their very own "Son of Texas." Not only did he bring fame and glory to the U.S. and to Kilgore in particular, but his performance in Moscow did more to ease the cold war tensions between the two world super powers than all of the ambassadors and politicians in the entire US Government.

Van Cliburn has performed for every American President since Harry Truman and for royalty and heads of state in Europe, Asia, and South America. In 1987, at the invitation of President Ronald Reagan he performed in the East Room of the White House during a State Visit honoring the Soviet Union General Secretary, Mikhail Gorbachev. His recording of Tchaikovsky's Concerto Number 1 sold more than a million copies during its first release. With his Van Cliburn Piano Competition held in Fort Worth every four years, he has done more to promote classical music and to recognize and encourage young musical artists than any single individual in America. Van Cliburn has been honored by outstanding universities all over the world, so it should come as no surprise that he has been adopted as a beloved son of Texas, entitled to all rights and privileges of a native born Texan, including "Texas Bragging rights" He is one of, if not THE greatest pianists, of all time. My wife and I have been very honored to have known Van Cliburn very well. He passed away not long ago and he will be sorely missed by classic music lovers around the world. WELL DONE VAN!!

Jim Rob "Bob" Wills, the "King of Western Swing" and composer of one of the most famous of Texas songs, "San Antonio Rose," was born at Turkey, Texas. Bob Wills and his "Texas Playboys" played with the "Light Crust Doughboys" of W. Lee "Pass the Biscuits Pappy" O'Daniel fame for a number of years. "San Antonio Rose" was broadcast into outer space for the

Apollo 12 Astronauts as they circled high above the earth.

Several other musical greats were born in Texas: Charles Hardin Holly, professionally known as Buddy Holly, the man that almost single handed pioneered rock and roll music, was born in Lubbock, Texas.

Roy Orbison was born in Vernon, Texas. In addition to writing and singing the famous hit song, Oh, Pretty Woman, he was the man who introduced John Lennon, Paul McCartney, George Harrison and Ringo Starr, to English audiences. They were later to be world famous as "The Beatles".

Texas also produced its fair share of country musicians. Among them, "Tex" Ritter, the "Singing Cowboy" was born in Nederland, Texas.

The famous actress, Debbie Reynolds, was born in El Paso, Texas.

Lucille Fay Leseur, better known as the famous movie actress, Joan Crawford, was born in San Antonio, Texas

Mary Martin, star of radio, stage and motion pictures, and the mother of Larry Hagman, star of the TV series "Dallas." was born at Weatherford, Texas.

Each of these individuals made a significant contribution to Texas, Texans and to America in general. Texas is honored to claim each of them as true born Native Texans!

CHAPTER 41

AND A FEW TEXAS TOWNS OF RENOWN

Fort Worth gained its fame first, as an army Fort. Following the construction of the railroads into Texas, Fort. Worth became a rail head for the shipment of cattle to the Eastern markets. Ranchers no longer had to make the arduous cattle drive to the rail head at Abilene, Kansas. They could ship their cattle from Fort Worth and save weeks on the trail drive and the stress and loss of cattle as they endured the drive. Fort Worth soon gained the nick name of "Cowtown". The huge cattle pens from which so many thousands of cattle were shipped still exist today. In its heyday, Fort Worth was a cattle man's and a cowboy's town. It was still several hundred miles from most of the large ranches to Fort Worth. Upon arrival with the large herds, cowboys wanted to celebrate and let off their pent-up steam and emotions. Fort Worth soon acquired a reputation for having a good place to do so, and that place was "Hells Half Acre". It was said to have the largest collection of bars, saloons, dance halls and brothels of any place south of Dodge City, Kansas. The wild side of life earned Ft. Worth the nickname of "The Paris of The Plains". Today Fort Worth vies with Dallas with its sophistication and culture.

Langtry, Texas is hardly a spot on the map of West Texas, yet it is famous. The town, if it can be called such, was originally named "Eagle's Nest Springs." As the railroad was being pushed westward through the God-forsaken West and lawless wilds north of Del Rio, Texas, the Texas Rangers decided they needed a local Justice of the Peace to whom they could entrust the care of their arrested miscreants so as to avoid the four hundred mile ride to Ft. Stockton. The Commissioners of Pecos County appointed Roy Bean Justice of the Peace with headquarters at Vinegeroon, Texas. Judge Roy Bean promptly pulled up stakes and moved his offices to a saloon at Eagle's Nest Springs. He renamed the "town" Langtry, Texas in honor of the then famous English Diva,

Lillie Langtry, with whom it was rumored, he was madly in love. At the time it was said that there was "no law west of the Pecos and no God west of El Paso." Judge Roy Bean immediately set out to cure the problem by administering his own style of justice. Roy Bean had a dubious background on both sides of the law and no "book learning" in the law. He soon created his own law known as the "Law West of the Pecos." He set up a table on the porch of his saloon and when it came time to administer justice, he shed his bar tender's apron, moved to the porch and listened to the evidence, using the butt of his six-shooter as a gavel. His verdicts were swift and sure, with the defendant's punishment administered right then and there. There is no record of Judge Bean actually hanging a villain, but he used his own crusty code of ethics as a yard stick by which to administer swift justice according to the "Law West of the Pecos". He once rendered his verdict for a man who was drunk and had fallen off a bridge and died with forty dollars in his pocket and a six gun in his belt. Judge Bean found that he should be fined forty dollars for carrying a loaded weapon. The fine covered his burial costs to the penny.

La Grange, Texas gained its reputation as the result of the movie "The Greatest Little Whorehouse in Texas." For many years La Grange was noted for an establishment located some few miles from town named "The Chicken Ranch." Like it's counterpart in Nevada, the "Mustang Ranch". It was a house of ill repute. Unlike the Mustang Ranch, the IRS never filed a lien on the Chicken Ranch nor had to take it over and operate it under the auspices of the "Internal Revenue Service" until it could be auctioned off. After considerable notoriety in several large city newspapers, the local sheriff felt compelled to close tha place down. Most Texans still wonder what the "service" of Internal Revenue Service means.

The small town of Edna gained national headlines through the fame of a beautiful stripper known by her stage name as "Candy Barr." "Candy" was born and reared in Edna. Following several years of notoriety, she was arrested and charged with prostitution. It was rumored that a number of husbands in and around Houston and Galveston spent a few sleepless nights for fear that Candy was going to make public a list of her "patrons."

More often than not, Texans can immediately recognize the general area of the state in which a person was born and reared by their accent. Different parts of the state have accents unique to that particular area. Along Highway 59, north of Houston, there is an area known as the "piney woods" of East Texas. To determine if a person is a bona-fide East Texan, especially if they are fifty years old or more, merely mention the names of two towns: "Teneha, Timpson", and their response will be "Bobo and Blair." The old timers recall when passenger trains plied the route between Houston and Texarkana. The Conductor would walk through the passenger cars calling out "next stop: Teneha, Timpson, Bobo and Blair", four small towns that were served by the railroad station at the town of Teneha. Try it some time on someone you suspect of being from East Texas and it is doubtful that you will be disappointed. My wife doubted my statement until one evening we were having dinner at the Grand Hyatt Hotel in New York City. Two couples sat down at the table adjacent to us. Based on their accents, I suspected that all four of them were from East Texas. I told my wife to pay close attention, that I was going to prove my point for all time. I asked our "neighbors" if they were from East Texas and they responded that "yes, they were from East Texas". I hesitated a moment then casually said "Tenaha, Timpson" and stopped. They all four immediately responded with "Bobo and Blair". My wife now takes me at my word!

CHAPTER 42

MORE TO TEXAS THAN WILD WEST LORE

Contrary to the generally accepted caricature of Texans, not all are cowboys or cowgirls and not every Texan wears cowboy boots with a tuxedo. However, the television series, "Dallas" was viewed by enough people around the world to have fostered that image. Cowboy boots and Stetson hats are standard attire for many, but, much like other Americans, Texans can also be found dressed in suits, casual clothes and bathing suits. At some professional football games you may note that there are many people who are obviously Texans, in the stands, dressed as you would expect Texans to dress; Stetson hats, cowboy boots and blue jeans. There may be a few dressed as foreigners in shorts, flip flops and tee shirts advertising various brands of beer. You may have also noticed some of the most beautiful cheer leaders in the world, most of whom are wearing various and sundry tiny bits of clothing along with the prerequisite Stetson Hat.

Football is an all consuming sport to most Texans, so perhaps we should start with a peek at how Texans prepare to enjoy a football game.

Tailgate parties at football games have become standard fare for many Texans. Such parties call for elaborate preparations. There will be the compulsory Bar-B-Q grill, along with cases and kegs of assorted brands of iced down beer. Folding chairs and camp stools with hordes of people, both male and female, gathered about their pickup trucks, most of whom have never previously met. A good and amiable time will be had by all regardless of which team each individual may be rooting for. This is called "Real Texas Hospitality." Some of the beer drinkers will also engorge propitious amounts of Bar-B-Que brisket and baby back ribs. At kick-off time, opposing fans will each go their own way and hopefully not see one another again until perhaps the next ball game where the process will be repeated all over again.

This may be an opportune time to point out that a Texas cowboy and a Dallas Cowboy are not one and the same. Most of the Dallas Cowboys, contrary to what some people may think, are not even from Texas. They are imported for the specific purpose of playing football just to entertain football crazed Texans, and occasionally, people in other parts of the world. It is rumored that several of the Dallas Cowboys are among the richest men in Texas. No such rumors abound about the "real Texas Cowboy". About the only thing the two have in common is that they both spend a great deal of time rolling around on the ground and taking a lot of physical abuse. And the "real Texas cowboy" performs without pads, helmets or other protective devises and for a lot less money.

Rodeos are another popular form of entertainment. Rarely do many of the fans at a rodeo know, nor have they ever previously heard, the names of the contestants. You can be sure however, that the vast majority of the fans will know the record to the second for barrel racing, calf roping, bronc and bull riding, and other rodeo events. They will vigorously applaud a good score and vigorously protest an unsportsmanlike attitude. If a barrel racing cowgirl, who are very rarely unseated, does happen to miss a turn around a barrel or a cowboy happens to be thrown by a mean bronc or a cantankerous bull and appears to be hurt, the silence is palatable until the condition of the contestant is known. If the contestant walks out of the arena under his own power and appears to be not seriously injured, then the crowd will erupt en-masse with applause. If he is unable to walk out pf the arena, a palatable huss will descend on the crowd. Texans love their rodeo cowboys and hope for a clean performance without any serious unjuries.

Rodeos, like football games are an exciting, but a relatively dangerous sport. Occasionally, there are serious injuries. At al of the Professional Rodeo Association rodeos, the contestants are professional rodeo participants. Most of the rodeo cowboys have some rodeo experience behind them. The skills practiced in professional rodeos are skills that were and, still are required of a cowboy to work cattle out in the real world. Performing against the clock at a rodeo requires a much higher and more precise level of various skills. That "clown fellow" that you notice running headlong into the face of a raging bull is trying to distract the bull to keep him from goring or trampling a thrown rider. There is only a flimsy barrel between him and that raging tornado. Or perhaps he is trying to get the attention of a wild "bronc" that has just thrown his worst enemy, the cowboy, who was trying to stay on his back for eight whole seconds. The bronc is pitching, pawing the ground and trying his best, once he has dislodged the cowboy, to get rid of the rope or strap tied around his belly that induces him to buck, and, given the chance, to do bodily harm to the cowboy, who had been crazy enough to believe he could master such an animal in the first place. It is the Rodeo Clown who is the real "hero" of this extravaganza. Without him, rodeos would be even less humane than the contests between the Christians and the Lions in the Coliseum in Rome during ancient times. To Texans, Rodeos are the ultimate contest between man and beast, and may the best man, (or beast), win! If the animal wins, there might be some severely damaged pride and a few broken bones and gashes here and there for the cowboy, but there will be no hard feelings for having been bested if the animal wins. Just wait until next time!!!

CHAPTER 43

RIDING INTO THE SUNSET

"Working" the cattle at the gathering pens is still done by cowboys on horseback much as it has been done for over two hundred years. Roping and branding still requires the expertise of a good "cutting" horse and an experienced cowboy. Watching a good cutting horse and his cowboy working a steer out of a herd of cattle is like watching a beautiful ballet performed on stage, just minus the "tutu". Proof of the expertise and unspoken communication between a cowboy and his horse is best demonstrated at the various rodeos and cutting horse shows. At a rodeo, it is a thing of beauty to watch a pair of cowboys and their horses "heading and heeling." To the uninitiated, "heading and heeling" requires that the first cowboy and his horse rope a four hundred pound streak of greased lightning by its head or horns and the second cowboy, immediately follow rope this same bolt of lightening by the hind legs, thereby stretching the now crazed animal out on the ground so that he can be branded on his flank. In rodeo competition the second cowboy is required to tie the calf's four legs with a "pigging string" and the team is judged in seconds from the time the calf breaks the line at the gate and the second cowboy puts both hands high in the air to show that he has done his job.

No actual branding is done at the rodeo; that chore is left for the real cowboy in real life. It is hard, hot, and demanding work, for both man and horse. In real life. depending upon the number of calves to be branded, a cowboy may wear out two or three horses in a morning or afternoon. The horse is the only participant that gets any rest. There are few such chores left for the "real cowboy". Most are done by mechanical devices, such as "squeeze chutes" and other methods of controlling the animal while it is being branded or vaccinated. Cattle ranching has declined with the innovation of new breeding techniques and the advent of the huge cattle feed lots, along with the importation of beef from Argentina, Brazil, and Australia, just to name a few other beef producing countries.

Real working Texas cowboys are a dying breed. The use of helicopters to round up cattle has proven to be faster and more practical than the old fashioned cowboy on horseback. Most of the "stick jockeys" are Vietnam veteran pilots; very good at what they do and addicted to flying helicopters. There is the beneficial aspect of putting less stress on the cattle. A good helicopter pilot can round up a herd of several hundred cattle within a matter of hours, steering them to the gathering pens by the shortest route. The same chore would take a couple of days of hard riding by several cowboys.

Millions of acres of Texas land and thousands of head of cattle were bought and sold based on a man's word and sealed by a handshake. Unfortunately, some land owners never got around to registering legal title to their land, especially those leagues of land granted to the Mexican settlers along and north of the Rio Grande by the King of Spain and later Mexico. In later years this resulted in a windfall for lawyers and land grabbers. The original owner's descendants many years later, discovered that they didn't legally own the land after all, because their titles hadn't been registered at the county courthouse. There are still battles raging in Texas courts over the rightful ownership of hundreds, if not thousands, of acres of South Texas land. This is especially true of some of the lands along the Rio Grande and the Gulf coast. Ownership of much of the land on South Padre Island has been in dispute for decades. Richard King, founder of the famous King Ranch, once thought he had purchased the southern half of South Padre Island, only to discover that the title he was given for the land was bogus and worthless.

In the late nineteenth and early twentieth century, most Texas ranches were figured in leagues and later in sections of land. A majority of the section lines in Texas drawn by survey lines are not "square" with the compass. In the days before modern methods of navigation for aviators, the deviation of the section lines from true north caused considerable trouble for pilots attempting to navigate by dead reckoning with only his compass and his visual orientation to guide him.

To ask a Texas rancher how many acres of land he owned, or how many cattle he owned, would often be taken as prying into his affairs. An insult guaranteed to bring a silent rebuke from the rancher. In many cases he wasn't sure himself. Courtesy and hospitality are always important to a Texan. He will make every effort to be courteous, but uninformative. The most likely answer to such a question would be something like this: "Waal now, you know this used to all be open range, then it got fenced and cross fenced. A feller could ride south from here about a day or day and a half and you'd come to an old mesquite tree that'd been struck by lightning, then turn east and ride a couple of days and you'll come to an old dry lake bed. From the center of that lake bed you'd turn north-north east for about a day, day and a half, where you'll find an old line shack, that is if it ain't blown down by now, then north 'bout a half days ride, then if you got your directions right you'll be back where you started. Its all mine. You ever back in these parts again, you come see me now, you hear." A firm hand shake and you're left scratching your hard head.

Trusting men to keep their word is a tradition that was part and parcel of being a Texan as far back as Texas history is recorded. This is not to infer that there were no scoundrels in Texas who would look you in the eye balls and make promises they had no intention of keeping, or tell someone a falsehood that would benefit him. In Texas as well as other states, we have bad apples mixed in with the majority of the good ones. Failure of a man to keep his word or to deal dishonestly with a neighbor is a sure way to earn the disgust and enmity of a Texan.

In the late nineteenth century, dozens of South Texas ranchers, sent tens of thousands of Longhorn cattle north to the railhead in Abilene, Kansas over the Chisholm Trail. Ownership of the cattle was transferred to the head Drover with a promise and a handshake. The rancher advanced sufficient funds to cover the expenses of the cattle drive. The cattle were sold at Abilene, the Drover collected the price of the cattle and returned to Texas to settle up with "The Boss". The entire transaction was completed without a scrap of paper or signature. (The Internal Revenue Service had not yet taken over people's lives and lawyers hadn't yet gotten up the nerve to invade the wilds of Texas, so people trusted one another). There is no record or even a rumor that either one failed to perform as promised.

Even though the era lasted only about twenty years, the famous cattle drives over the old Chisholm

Trail and the Loving-Goodnight Trail during the late 1800's, sparked the imagination of millions of people the world over. Drovers moved several thousand head of cattle in a herd to the rail head at Abilene, Kansas, battling the terrain, the elements, and often, the Indians who were intent upon getting away with as many cattle as they could, either by killing or maiming the cowboys guarding the herd. Generations of children in America and around the world have grown up reading about the Texas cowboy and his exploits and listening to songs and ballads of his "Home on the Range", "Back in the Saddle Again", and dozens of other nostalgic songs by the "singing cowboys," Gene Autry, Tom Mix, Roy Rogers and a host of others. These were the old time Saturday afternoon matinee idols of our more recent past history. As a result, a mystique has developed about the Texas cowboy. The era of the idolized cowboy is long gone, but their legacy as true Texans lives on.

Cowboys and "wannabe" cowboys are big on pick-up trucks and dogs. You will notice that they are partial to Chevys and Fords. Until recent years, no foreign trucks for these "good old boys". Most generally you will find a rifle or two in a rack across the back window. Whether or not he has any cattle or even works for a rancher, a cowboy might have a coiled rope hanging from his "head ache rack", a couple of sacks of feed, and possibly a bale of hay in the bed of the truck. Perched in the bed of the truck will likely be a dog. It will probably be either a "Lab" or a "Blue Heeler" cow dog. His dog will be trained to jump into the truck upon his master's command, perch his fore feet on the railing of the truck bed, stick his head out about two feet into the wind with his tongue hanging out in obvious bliss, and bark at anything or anybody that happens to catch his attention. He will wait patiently in the truck for his master at the feed store, service station, café or the beer joint. No amount of enticement by a stranger can make him budge from that truck. Approaching too close can often result in a mangled hand or arm, so don't try it no matter how placid the dog may seem! These "good old boys" will very likely stop and help you change a flat tire, jump start your engine if your battery is down, go down the road a mile or two and bring you a couple of gallons of gasoline if you need it, or just stop and say "howdy" and mean it.

Texas is much more than cows, cowboys, horses, and ranching. Today, Texas cities rank near the top of the list in the arts; music, opera, the legitimate theater, sports and entertainment of all kinds. Prior to World War II, the social, economic and industrial center of the United States was centered in the North and Northeast areas of the United
States. The Texas economy was driven primarily by farming, ranching, petroleum and its related industries. With the outbreak of World War II, Texas had all of the necessary resources to gear up and supply the war effort.

Once Texas began to become industrialized, there was no stopping its progress.

Education has always been extremely important to Texans. That is not to say that all Texans believe that every young man or woman is a budding "rocket scientist," although Texas has produced several of those too. Texas abounds with technical schools and junior colleges. Rocket scientists, doctors, lawyers, university professors, accountants and dozens of other professions require "back up people" to support not only their professions but also their everyday lives. There must be plumbers, mechanics, electricians, and a host of other vocations to sustain our homes and our lives. Fortunately, Texas has always had a high standard of dedication for teachers, instructors and professors. Texas abounds in state supported universities and privately endowed and religious-supported universities. Rice University has long been considered the "Harvard of the South" and very favorably compared with Oxford

University of England. The University of Texas, with a huge enrollment at Austin and thousands more at their subsidiary branches throughout the state, has the finest medical research hospitals in the United States. The University of Texas Transplant Center in San Antonio, a part of the UT Health Science Center, is world renowned, especially for kidney research and kidney transplant and liver transplant and research. Methodist Hospital, Cardiac Care Center, and Cancer Research Center and Organ Transplant Center in San Antonio is the finest in the world. St. Luke's Hospital, M. D,. Anderson Cancer Center and the Texas Medical Center of Houston are world renowned. A center where patients come from all corners of the world for treatment. Southern Methodist University in Dallas and Saint Marys University in San Antonio are home to two famous law Schools. Texas A&M University at College Station with its huge ROTC program and engineering programs has produced some of the finest graduates that have become leaders in our military service and engineers of world renown. A&M is known world-wide for its research and accomplishments in agricultural development. Millions of people in third world countries are benefiting from A and M's agricultural research that has doubled food production world wide

Texas Tech University at Lubbock, Baylor University at Waco, Texas Christian University, at Lubbock, Sul Ross University of Alpine, are all top ranked Universities in the United States. There are a host of other universities, colleges and technical schools throughout Texas that serve its citizens within a very short drive of all population centers of the state.

Texas and Texans are in the vanguard of science and technology. Our medical institutions and our doctors and scientists are tackling the plague of cancer, strokes and heart desease, and are making outstanding progress. In 1975, I had a major heart attack. I was suffering from arterioscleroses and my only hope was to have surgical bypasses of those arteries, an operation that required the opening of the chest for access to the heart, and the use of a heart-lung machine to allow the heart to be stopped during the surgery. It was a relatively new procedure and was considered very risky. When one's life hangs in the balance, the decision becomes easier to make. The one and only hospital and the one surgical team with the facilities and expertise to perform such an operation at that time was St. Luke's Hospital in Houston and the surgical team headed by the noted cardiovascular surgeon, Dr. Denton Cooley and his assistants. The surgery was performed without incident. I spent a few days in recovery and within a month I was completely recovered, only in better health than before. Today such surgery is routine and is done in hundreds of hospitals and by hundreds of surgeons around the world. I required the same surgery again in 1990. That surgery also went through without incident but my recovery time was weeks less than my first surgery and the surgery was done at our local hospital.

Doctor Denton Cooley is a true Texan and a hero to thousands of heart patients around the world. Royalty and members of royal families from numerous countries have chosen to come to Texas for surgery and treatment, not only for heart disease, but cancer and many of the other ailments that plague mankind. Texas and Texans will continue to be pioneers just as they did when they conquered the wilds of Texas.

Texas has an abundance of the most talented experts in their fields known to man. Texas has built and is still building facilities to accomplish wonders that our fore bearers never envisioned. And, with God's help, we will continue to do so.

The old frontiers that challenged Texans and others in the previous centuries were fraught with physical dangers that our ancestors encountered. We have new frontiers to conquer. Texans have already shown their ability to adapt to the changes required in the new century. Texas and Texans have been in the forefront of the space age. While it may appear that we have conquered space by building and manning the International Space Station in concert with the Russians and others, we have hardly "scratched the surface," in a matter of speaking. At this immediate time, right now, serious plans and efforts are underway to construct a Space Port near the gulf coast in South Texas, anticipating the launch of from right here in Texas. Huge Wind Farms have already been constructed in West Texas and new sites near the gulf coast, where winds are favorable, are under construction.

In the final analysis I have held to the belief that Texans really are different in many respects from other Americans. That belief has been verified and reinforced. It is not that we awakened early one morning and just decided that we "are going to be different". Our differences are not self imposed, but are the result of many factors. The genes of our ancestors that are a part of our heritage is just one of those factors. Our pride and self esteem in the knowledge that they accomplished the near impossible is a result of the experiences that their forefathers instilled in them and they in us. They passed down to us in the later generations, the knowledge that through their experiences the impossible just takes a bit longer and requires a lot of hard work Those ancestors that preceded us left us with a legacy that as Texans we are bound to uphold: We will honor our obligation to protect our land and our homes. Texans will resist to the best of their ability the incursion of outside interference in the life and conduct of the business of their state and their community. They will resist with all of their might any attempt by foreign or outside forces to dominate or to control their personal beliefs and way of life. A Texan will generally welcome friends from wherever they may come to join with them in peace and prosperity, free to live as they choose, within the law, so long as they respect the Texan's way of life as they do their own. These dreams and aspirations are not really so different from the dreams and aspirations of most other American, either Native born or Nationalized. Most of the defining traits of all Americans are traits that we Texans share in abundance. We resist any domination from or by any source. We, as do most Americans, ask only that we be allowed to manage our own affairs as we deem appropriate and fit, without interference from outsiders, either in our personal, political lives or our economic well being. These are personality traits that our ancestors handed down to us. They sweated, shed blood, fought and died to create what we call Texas. They paid a high price for it. Now it is up to us, descendants of those pioneers, to carry on the traditions that made us who we are.

Texas is one of only a few states that has no personal income tax. It has a very low tax on corporations. As a result Texas has attracted thousands of manufacturing and service corporations to the state. Texas has a Right to Work Law, allowing employees to either join a union or not. It is their individual choice.

Texans are proud of their state. A first impression could be that Texans are arrogant. Nothing could be further from the truth. Texans are well aware of the possibility of a few native Texans' short comings. They don't hesitate to talk about themselves and their State. They are just a bit defensive when outsiders bring up undeserved criticisms about their beloved state. .When disaster strikes in other states, or even foreign countries, Texans are among the first volunteers to mobilize and go to the scene to give all of the assistance they can. Two such incidents come to mind: The oil field tragedies in Kuwait during and after the Gulf War and the devastating loss of life and property damage inflicted on the Gulf Coast by the hurricane "Katrina". Before the call for help went out, Texans were already gearing up to go and give of their time, expertise and fortune.

I do not pretend to offer proof that any of my assumptions, or in many cases my opinions, are valid, but, like most other "Texas Old Coots," I hope that my descendents will continue the fight for our right to be "who we are" until "all Texas rivers run north and hell freezes over". It has been said that often men are rarely appreciated in their own time and in their own country. I have found that Texans in their individuality are truly appreciated wherever they go, at home or abroad. If we continue to follow the traditions of our ancestors, it will continue to be so. Although, as I have pointed out, I am not a typical Texan, nor do I know anyone who truly is typical; Texans will continue to be "Texans" so long as the blood of those who have gone before us continues to flow in our veins.

There are signs along our highways with the message: "Don't Mess With Texas." These signs are referring to messing up our highways and roads with trash and litter, not directed toward anyone nor do they mean anything personal, except, that is, don't "mess with Texas" by littering our highways and parks. Residents and civic organizations volunteer to clean our highways and road right-of-ways of litter and trash. They merely want to call to everyone's attention that it is unl-AWFUL to litter Texas Highways and Byways. We really are who we are and what we are because "We Are Texans".

AFTERWORD

Texans are proud not only of their state, but are equally as proud to be Americans and a part of American history. Since the beginning of the industrial revolution, and even before, every major power in the world but one, has attempted to colonize territories outside the sphere of their immediate borders. The British Empire became the largest empire in the world. It was said with pride by the British that "The sun never sets on the British Empire". And that statement was true for many years. France colonized a great deal of Africa and part of South-East Asia, and even some parts of the New World along with Holland, Germany, and Portugal, who set up several of their own colonies in Africa. Spain had her colonies in the Caribbean and on the American continent, including what is now Texas , but she failed to recognize the one opportunity that could have made her greater than any other nation in the world. She let her desire for riches be stronger than the desire to spread her influence through the burdensome responsibility of establishing colonies of her people in the New World. Of course one would have to assume that Spanish settlers would be as industrious as the English, Scots, and Scots-Irish turned out to be for such a thought to be within the realm of possibility. The only major nation that has been strong politically, economically and militarily that has never made any effort to colonize any other part of the world, has been the United States of America. We have become the most powerful nation on earth, yet we have never made any effort, politically, economically or militarily, to dominate, subjugate or possess any territory beyond our own borders. Any expansion of soil by our country has been by fair and open purchases; the Louisiana Purchase and Alaska. Any other expansion has been through the desire of the residents as happened when Hawaii became our 50th state. For the safety and welfare of Guam and Puerto Rico, for example, we have taken the responsibility to protect both islands while allowing them to enjoy all of the freedoms and benefits of America. The American people have never shown any desire to dominate any other nation. We went to war with our neighbor, Mexico, after they had made many incursions onto American soil without provocation. Once we had convinced them to stay on their side of the border and try to be good neighbors, we withdrew all of our forces and left them in peace. We have been ready to go to the aid of other, smaller, and larger countries when asked to do so and we found that it was necessary to help them protect their freedoms. So, why is this? The best answer is that we are all Americans and that is just the way Americans are. Texans are unique but we are also Americans.

Now to set the historical record of Texas straight! I have read a couple of books, recently,(published within the past ten years), claiming that in the late 1800's, Texas was a "slave state", even before Texas was a

Republic or a state; Claiming that slaves and the cotton economy that depended on the slave labor, was the prime reason for Anglo settlers migrating to Texas. I have spent some time searching for anything that might lend any credence to this theory. It is PURE BUNK! The people who have written such books also put forth the claim that the Anglos "took" Texas away from the Mexicans after having introduced slavery into Northern Mexico. Another theory of PURE BUNK! Spain, France nor Mexico, ever made any legitimate effort to encourage settlers from their countries to settle any part of "Tejas", except for the small strip of land adjacent to the Rio Grande, because of their fear of the Indians. Once the Anglos made it safe to do so, some few Mexican settlers began moving farther into Texas.

Mexico had an army ten times larger, much better equipped and trained, than "Tejas", but Sam Houston put them to rout at San Jacinto, capturing their General of the Army/President, Santa Anna allowing him to survive and return to Mexico after, as President of Mexico, he legally ceded all of Texas to the Texans, a document by the way, that was found to be legally binding in 1846 by the World Court in Geneva, Switzerland.

Any such unfounded literary efforts as those put forth by these few uninformed "authors" should be shown up to be just what they are: PURE BUNK. We should not allow such wild and untrue theories to be taught in our schools.

THE END

Made in the USA
San Bernardino, CA
06 September 2016